**Fancy Drinks and Popular Beverages
by The Only William**

Published by:
IRLY Books,
7605 Maryknoll Avenue
Bethesda, MD 20817

Cover design by Paul Kraytman

ISBN 0-9766265-5-1

Printed in the United States of America

Reprint of the 1896 Edition

FANCY DRINKS

AND

POPULAR BEVERAGES

BY THE
ONLY WILLIAM.

FANCY DRINKS

AND

POPULAR BEVERAGES

HOW TO

PREPARE AND SERVE THEM

BY

THE ONLY WILLIAM

NEW YORK

DICK & FITZGERALD

Index.

(The Figures Indicate the Number of the Drink.)

FANCY DRINKS
AND
POPULAR BEVERAGES.

To those who do not find the following useful in its details for their own use, I express my congratulations and esteem as a business associate. To those who do find it a guide I wish to express my assurance that they will find this work an absolutely and indispensably correct one to work by, provided they understand and practice it.

You may travel all over the country, and you will find my practice a good one. In discharging your duties you will find many little hints you will not be able to practice for not having the facilities to do so, but I may say I have at least shown you how it ought to be made and executed. It must be left to your own judgment to follow the directions given herein the best way you know of, and leave out what ought to be left out, because your position does not offer you the opportunity. I have mentioned in this work everything that is necessary for a theoretical experience. It should be borne in mind: Not everybody can advance so as to become an artist in tending bar, but we all should learn, and try to improve by all means that are offered. I am far from believing it possible to become a practical man by simply studying this book, but while doing so, you will get an essential and true idea of how to become a valuable man in this line of business. Every man can educate himself and acquire all the knowledge necessary for tending bar, provided he takes enough interest and wants to make it a business. Practical knowledge cannot be acquired except by actual work and experience.

An inexpert cook never will become an artist nor a *chef de cuisine* by simply reading a book on cookery, no matter by whom or how intelligently written, and no man can ever become an artist behind the bar by simply looking into this book or possessing it. A great deal of ingenuity and taste is required on the part of a *chef* in an important position, and the same is required on the part of a man in the capacity of a bartender. He, having a position of responsibility, must be a man of original ideas, a man who is proud of his work and who tries to discharge his duties with credit to himself, his employer, and the guest he waits on. Originality is the key to success. Therefore, always try to work accordingly; make a change in the old system, if you see it needs improvement; introduce it to your guests instead of being taught by them what to do. A bartender ought to be leading and not to be led. An actor must understand for himself how to amuse his audience and how to gain a reputation: he never would succeed by simply following another man's guidance.

The situation of a barkeeper gives the holder the chance of studying human nature. A man fit for the position, and consequently a keen observer—for one thing cannot be separated from the other—will be able to tell a man's character very soon, as far as conduct, education, language, and general *savoir-vivre* are concerned.

Such a situation is a better teacher of human nature than any book howsoever, and by whomsoever it may be written. " Tell me what you drink and I will tell you who you are." The tastes and habits of your different customers appear to you so plain, that you have to take an interest in this study of human nature.

As a general rule you will find that only a little part of drinking is done by one individual. A gentleman either brings his company with him or he expects to find it in the barroom. It is in drinking as it is in eating: very few want to enjoy their drinks by themselves.

As to my individual belief, all men are born equal, with a heart full of honesty; I cannot believe any one might think otherwise. If any one grows up to become different, it is the fault of his surroundings or his own carelessness. How any one can lie without knowing what he does it for, I cannot comprehend. Thus with me! Many a time I have been asked concerning mixed drinks: What do you think of them in regard to their effect and result to the stomach ? Many a time I have heard the complaint, mixed drinks make a person sick; consequently we do not believe in them; we think them to be bad and a failure. Patience, my dear patrons ! Most cheerfully I give the following answer: Drinking is a luxury, water and milk excepted, and any man will admit this fact who is not a slave to drinking. First of all, if you make a mixed drink, your honesty must force you to use pure articles only. Suppose you need for your drink three or four ingredients; take every article genuine but one, and you will spoil the entire drink by the one that is not genuine. Therefore, order mixed drinks only in reliable places.

Secondly: Never order a mixed drink when you are in a hurry; you can get a well-mixed drink only when you devote the time absolutely necessary to prepare it.

Thirdly: The mixer ought to be careful not to use too much of one ingredient and too little of another. Do not get too much water in your drink when you prepare drinks with ice; find the suitable temperature, not too warm nor too cold; chiefly, however, be careful in your measurements, and compare a plain drink in its size with your mixed one.

Mixing drinks might be compared to music; an orchestra will produce good music, provided all players are artists; but have only one or two inferior musicians in your band, and you may be convinced they will spoil the entire harmony.

A man who is a slave to drinking will always prefer something strong, even if less palatable, and the effect is generally harmful to his brain; whereas the man who believes in mixed drinks may hurt his stomach, in case he drinks too much; but even this too much will never reach the quantity of the former.

It must be borne in mind: Drinking is an art, and it requires practice to know how to drink, what to drink, and when to drink. Drinking is like eating. Who but a cannibal would not prefer his viands prepared in a palatable form? That fancy cooking is not injurious, we have full proof of; we know of aged people of the past and of the present who spent a little fortune in having their dishes made to suit their taste. As good eating depends on the cook, so good drinking on the expert barkeeper.

A distinguished Englishman, Mr. T., one day told me: "We do not have much mixed drinks in our country." Whereupon I asked him: "Why do your countrymen mix ale with porter, or Bass ale with ginger ale?" "Well, it makes the drink more pleasant to the taste." I needed no more answer.

A man gets tired of good company, of good friends, or even of his best girl—why should we wonder at seeing him getting tired of mixed drinks? I cannot help stating the fact that our drinking capacity is increasing, compared with former times. Not everybody is capable of criticising and appreciating a good drink, more so a mixed one. Never smoke when you want to enjoy a fine drink, nor chew; never drink anything mixed when you do not feel well. For medical purposes, plain drinks are preferable.

When I began my business as bartender, I was only a boy and hardly able to keep up with the demands of my employer; I remembered this often enough afterwards; yet the imagination on my part was at that time like that of the rest of boys of the same age. But with the advance in age, this imagination faded, for it had to; and now I began to learn. A period of a few years passed and I began to believe I knew something; undoubtedly I did, but how little! and every day convinces me more and more how much there is to be learned, although I have given particular care to this business close on to thirty years.

How often a man will overestimate himself, because he happens to be successful, as well as another one will undervalue his dexterity because good luck did not favor him. Perhaps you think I was born with a fortune waiting for me; I was, but I was not to keep it, and only my misfortune in younger years is the cause, and has ever since been, that made me work hard and seek new ideas. There is no more reason for a well-off man to give up his ambition than there is for another, who did not meet with success, to despair. Surely it is a nice, pleasant feeling for any one to be born rich; but to be born with a silver spoon in the mouth and to die with a fortune behind you, without having shown that you accomplished something of value through your daily toils and labors—no! I would rather be a dog than a man without ambition and a record of toil.

My dear readers! Never was I guilty of not enjoying myself at every opportunity after business hours, and I never will let the time pass by without doing so hereafter. It is a pleasure to me to enjoy the labor, the skill and the talent of others, and I know how to value and appreciate it, but still my greatest pleasure is to amuse others; and you will find, " True happiness is gained by making others happy." Often have I done extra work to amuse my friends, for the pleasure I felt was ample reward.

I would mention right here some of my little extra doings, different from the usual way. When you are not pushed for time, while you are making mixed drinks, cool your glasses with ice before you serve your drink; in serving a strained drink, you begin with serving a glass of ice-water; then fill your glass, into which you are to strain your drink, with ice. You may place your glasses together in the form of a pyramid and ornament your structure with fruits and flowers. Now begin to prepare your drink. By following these hints you will accomplish several purposes : Firstly, you will please the eye of your customer; secondly, you will have thoroughly cooled glasses; thirdly, you will not need to wipe your glasses dry, etc.

On a hot summer day you will find such little extras to a great advantage to the business practically, *i. e.*, financially. A drink well served is worth two that lack in presentation.

When a drink is made with ice and then strained, there should be nothing left in the glass but the liquid; the fruit would hinder you in drinking, it would touch the mustache; if you want to eat it you cannot get it out, and the fruit has lost its natural aroma; fruit ought, consequently, to be presented separately, if it is desired on your guest's part.

Very different it is when you have a drink in which the ice is to remain; in this case use plenty of fruits, as it is pleasing to the eye and allows your guest to eat it if he likes.

Reasons Why Men Drink.

MEN drink to quench thirst, on account of a drink's effect, to get an appetite, to promote digestion, to enjoy its taste, for curiosity, from habit, because of discouragement, on account of ambition, to forget poverty, to show their riches, because of sickness, because they do not feel well, for the purpose of learning, to dispel sorrow. This one wants to warm himself; that one is overheated and wants to get cool; one has lost in Wall Street; another's shares have gone up; one man's best girl went back on him; another is going to marry the best girl in town; one drinks behind the door, another in a public place. Some men will drink out of pure style; they want to show their diamonds and jewelry, their costly clothes, and mainly their money. But most men will drink because it is " business." I remember a circumstance that occurred between a diamond broker of Maiden Lane and myself. One fine morning a customer entered his store to buy goods, but the broker did not succeed in selling, when all at once the idea struck him, "A nice drink might bring him to terms." He invited his customer and up they came to the bar. With a twinkle in his eye he ordered " Two of those famous Sans Soucis." I went to work and built up the glasses, à l'Eiffel tower, with all the necessary fruits and flowers, and after having received a pleasant compliment from my guest, I saw them going down to the store once more. As I was afterwards informed, the broker sold his customer $10,000 worth of goods with ease.

How to Start.

CLEAN the top of your counter first, remove all utensils from under the counter and place them on the top; clean your bench. Before beginning with your glassware, add a little salt to the water as it will help in polishing your glasses. Fill all your liquor bottles, pack your working boxes with fine ice, cut up the fruit for immediate use, clean your silverware. Fill your ice-boxes with ice. Afterward clean your back bar.

As an appropriate suit behind the bar I would mention the following: a pair of black trousers, a long, white apron, a white shirt, a white collar, a black tie, a white vest, and a white coat; care should be taken to have the suit fit well; have the sleeves of your coat cut, that you may button it tight; this will prevent its getting soiled and worn out; never have your suit starched.

Glassware.

IN selecting your glassware, choose perfectly white color, also for your bottles, as they look much more inviting. To keep them clean, use egg-shells, salt, paper, or chopped ice. It should be remembered that shot is very poisonous and scratches the glass. Soda ought also to be avoided. Use only plain but good glass-ware, it being the best.

Fruits.

Lemons.—Lemons intended for squeezing should be peeled before using. The juice ought not to be older than a day. It must be strained thoroughly. Lime-juice may be mixed with lemon-juice; the mixture is cheaper and better. The fresh lemon-peel is very useful for flavoring and decorating the drinks.

Oranges.—A medium size of dark-colored ones is the best for squeezing, as well as cutting up. Use from six to twelve oranges, according to the demand of the business; peel them and take them apart carefully; place them in a punch-bowl, add some fine sugar, pour either Rhine wine, sherry wine or brandy over it; let it stand in a cold place from three to six hours, and serve a piece to your customer after the drink, and you will find it will be appreciated.

The Delicious Pineapple.—Pineapple may be used in the same way as oranges, the juice or syrup being al-most indispensable.

Choice Grapes.—To make a drink of inviting appear-ance choice grapes are necessary, for decorating as well as simply presenting.

In addition to these fruits, a few others ought to be

kept on hand: Strawberries, raspberries, blackberries and cherries.   They may be prepared the same way as the other fruits.

Never handle fruits with your fingers, but use a fancy fruit-fork.

Canned Fruits.

AT a time when there are no fresh fruits to be had, canned goods may be taken instead of them. The juice or the syrup of them lends a very aromatic flavor to drinks—such as cobblers, punches, sours, fizzes and lemonades.   You also may present a little of these fruits to your customers.

To persons who drink strong liquors, the use of fruits is of a much greater advantage than lunch.   The proper way of serving such little relishes is to put them in a separate little glass, or present on a fork or a toothpick.

Further Instructions.

NEVER allow yourself to be idle behind the bar; be ready to serve at once when a customer enters.   When a drink is ordered that requires water, fill your glass with fine ice, and pour over it water out of a pitcher in full view of your guest.   This rule must necessarily be carried out in performing every one of your duties.   A bottle never must be more than half empty. For strong drinks, always serve two glasses—one for the drink, the other for the water.   Serve sherry and port wine in their respective glasses only; never do it in whiskey tumblers.

For shaking drinks with the shaker, use only a mixing-tumbler; by using goblets you will soil your clothes, and the goblets might break. Shake your drink well; without that you never will get a first-class drink. This has special reference to such drinks as fizzes, milk punches, egg-noggs, frappés, and similar drinks, containing sugar. Good mixing is a hard work; but without good mixing you spoil the best liquor.

As we mention syrup or gum so often, we think it a necessity to call your attention to the way **of** making and using it.

Take an enameled pot, of about half a gallon; put in this one and a half quarts of water and two pounds of loaf-sugar; let this boil over a slow fire; stir now and then, and skim well; if too thick, add a little boiling water, and strain into a bottle. It ought to be kept in a cold place. Do not prepare too large quantities, as it is best to have it fresh.

Rock - candy gum is prepared in the same way. Cocktail gum should be absolutely white.

Mixed Drinks.

1. Jack Frost Whiskey Sour.

Into a mixing-glass squeeze the juice of half a lemon,
> 1 barspoonful of sugar,
> 1 fresh egg,
> 1 pony of fresh cream,
> 1 drink of apple whiskey.

Fill your glass with cracked ice and shake thoroughly; strain into a high, thin glass, and fill the balance with imported seltzer.

2. Sour à la Créole.

The juice of a large lime in a large glass,
> a barspoonful of fine sugar,
> a dash of seltzer; mix this well;
> ½ drink of Santa Cruz rum,
> ½ drink of Jamaica rum.

Mix this well, fill your glass with fine ice, ornament with fruits in season, put a little ice-cream on top, and serve.

3. Whiskey Sour à la Guillaume.

A large glass with fine ice,
> the juice of half a lemon,
> 3 dashes of gum,
> a drink of whiskey,
> 2 spoonfuls of cream.

Shake this, strain, and serve.

4. The Delicious Sour.

A goblet with the juice of a lime,
             a squirt of seltzer,
             a spoonful of sugar,
             ½ of apple-jack,
             ½ of peach brandy,
             the white of an egg.
Fill your glass with ice, shake well, strain, and serve.

5. Oriental Brandy Sour.

Into a mixing-glass squeeze the juice of half a lemon,
             a barspoonful of sugar,
             the juice of half an orange,
             the white of an egg,
             a drink of peach brandy.
Fill the glass with cracked ice, shake to the freezing-point,
strain into a fancy glass, and serve.

6. Whiskey Sour.

A goblet with the juice of half a lemon or lime in the bottom,
             a squirt of seltzer,
             a little sugar; mix this;
             ⅔ full of ice,
             a drink of whiskey; mix this well.
Strain, and serve.

7. Whiskey Daisy.

It is made as a whiskey sour; only put a dash of some cordial
on top, such as chartreuse or curaçao.

8. Absinthe Cocktail.

A goblet of shaved ice,
>2 dashes of maraschino,
>1 dash of bitters (orange),
>1 dash of anisette,
>1 pony of absinthe.

Stir very well, strain into a cocktail glass, and serve.

9. The Angelus.

Fill a large glass two-thirds full of fine ice,
>1 dash of gum,
>1 dash of absinthe,
>a little vino vermouth,
>1 pony of Old Tom gin,
>2 dashes of orange bitters,
>2 dashes of curaçao.

Stir well, and strain into a fancy glass.

10. The Anticipation.

A glass with fine ice,
>1 dash of absinthe,
>2 dashes of gum,
>½ of sherry wine,
>½ of vino vermouth.

Freeze this well; strain and serve.

11. The Bitter-Sweet Cocktail.

A glass with ice,
>⅓ drink of kümmel,
>⅓ drink of vino vermouth,
>4 dashes of absinthe,
>1 dash of bitters (orange),
>3 dashes of gum,
>1 dash of anisette.

Stir, strain, and serve.

12. The Great Appetizer.

Fill a glass with ice,
3 dashes of gum,
½ pony of absinthe,
2 dashes of bitters (calisaya),
1 dash of orange bitters,
1 dash of vino vermouth.

Stir this well, strain, and serve.

13. Bon-Appetit.

A goblet two-thirds full of fine ice,
2 dashes of gum,
1 dash of bitters,
1 dash of absinthe,
⅔ of vino vermouth,
⅓ of sherry wine.

Stir well, strain, and serve.

14. Appetizer à l'Italienne.

⅔ of vino vermouth,
⅓ of Fernet branca,
1 dash of absinthe,
2 dashes of gum.

A little ice in the glass, stir well, strain, and serve.

15. L'Aurore.

A goblet filled with fine ice,
1 dash of gum,
2 dashes of orange bitters,
⅓ of vino vermouth,
⅔ of Old Tom gin,
1 dash of absinthe,
1 dash of maraschino.

Stir, strain, and serve with a little fruit.

16. The Beginner.

A goblet with fine ice,
>> 2 dashes of gum,
>> 2 dashes of orange bitters,
>> 1 dash of absinthe,
>> ½ of French vermouth,
>> ½ of Russian kümmel.

Stir this well, strain, and serve.

17. The Brain-Duster.

Into a mixing-tumbler squeeze the juice of a lime,
>> 2 dashes of gum,
>> 1 pony of absinthe,
>> 2 dashes of vino vermouth,
>> 2 dashes of sherry wine.

Fill your glass with ice, stir, strain, and serve.

18. Exquisite.

A goblet with 2 dashes of gum,
>> 1 dash of bitters,
>> 1 dash of absinthe,
>> ⅔ of vino vermouth,
>> ⅓ of Russian kümmel,
>> 1 dash of crême de roses.

Fill your glass with ice, stir, strain, and serve.

19. The First One.

A goblet with fine ice,
>> 2 dashes of gum,
>> ½ pony of crême de menthe,
>> 1 pony of Old Tom gin,
>> 1 dash of orange bitters.

Squeeze the juice of a lemon-peel to it; stir well, strain, and serve.

20. The Gladstone.

Fill a tumbler half-full with fine ice,
2 dashes of gum,
a little maraschino,
2 dashes of bitters,
1 dash of absinthe,
1 drink of whiskey,
1 dash of Jamaica rum,
1 dash of Russian kümmel.
Stir well and strain into a cocktail glass.

21. Holland Gin Cocktail.

A goblet filled with fine ice,
2 dashes of gum,
1 dash of absinthe,
1 drink of Holland gin,
2 dashes of orange bitters.
(1 dash of green chartreuse may be added.)
Stir this well, strain, and serve.

22. Holland's Pride.

A mixing glass ⅔ full of ice,
3 dashes of gum,
2 dashes of bitters,
1 dash of absinthe,
⅔ of Holland gin,
⅓ of vino vermouth.
Stir well, strain, and serve.

23. Manhattan Cocktail.

Half a tumblerful of cracked ice,
2 dashes of gum,
2 dashes of bitters,
1 dash of absinthe,
⅔ drink of whiskey,
⅓ drink of vino vermouth.
(A little maraschino may be added.)
Stir this well, strain, and serve.

24. Imperial Opal.

A mixing-glass ⅔ filled with fine ice,
>
>1 pony of absinthe,
>1 dash of anisette,
>1 dash of chartreuse (yellow).

Shake this to the freezing-point; strain into a cocktail glass; drop a little crême de roses in the centre, and serve

25. The Opal.

A goblet with ice,
>
>2 dashes of gum,
>1 pony of absinthe,
>1 dash of maraschino.

Stir well, strain into a cocktail glass; pour a little crême de menthe in the centre, which will go to the bottom, and serve.

26. The Preserver.

A large glass ⅔ full of fine ice,
>
>1 dash of bitters,
>1 dash of absinthe,
>⅔ of vino vermouth,
>⅙ of anisette,
>⅙ of curaçao.

Mix well, strain into a fancy glass, and present.

27. Soda Cocktail.

A large glass with a spoonful of sugar,
>
>squeeze a little oil of the peel of a lemon on it,
>a little fine ice,
>2 dashes of bitters.

Pour in a bottle of plain soda slowly with your left hand, while you stir it with your right hand, and present; strain if desired.

28. Tom Gin Cocktail.

A goblet filled with ice,
>   2 small dashes of gum,
>   1 dash of absinthe,
>   1 drink of Old Tom gin,
>   2 dashes of orange bitters.

(A dash of green chartreuse may be added.)
Stir well, strain, and serve.

29. Club Cocktail.

Half a glassful of ice,
>   2 dashes of gum,
>   ⅔ of Old Tom gin,
>   ⅓ of vino vermouth,
>   2 dashes of orange bitters,
>   1 dash of green chartreuse.

Stir well, strain, and serve.

30. Vermouth Cocktail.

A glass with some fine ice,
>   1 dash of bitters,
>   2 dashes of maraschino,
>   1 dash of absinthe,
>   1 drink of vino vermouth.

Stir to the freezing-point, and strain into a cocktail glass.

31. The Weeper's Joy.

A goblet ⅔ full of fine ice,
>   3 dashes of gum,
>   ½ pony of absinthe,
>   ½ pony of vino vermouth,
>   ½ pony of kümmel,
>   1 dash of curaçao.

Stir very well, and strain into a cocktail glass.

32. Whiskey Cocktail.

Half a glassful of fine ice,
>   squeeze a little lemon-peel over it,
>   3 dashes of gum,
>   2 dashes of bitters,
>   1 dash of absinthe,
>   1 drink of whiskey.

Stir this well, strain and serve.

33. Hot Apple Toddy.

A lump of sugar dissolved in half a glass of boiling water,
>   a drink of apple whiskey.

Add a piece of a roasted apple, if you wish, and serve with a little nutmeg.

34. Hot Beef-Tea.

Break an egg in the bottom of a cup; beat it well;
>   a drink of sherry,
>   a spoonful of beef-tea.

Fill the balance with boiling water; stir well, season to taste, and serve.

35. Hot Benefactor.

A hot punch-glass with 2 or 3 lumps of sugar,
>   ½ glass of boiling water to dissolve,
>   ⅔ of Chianti,
>   ⅓ of Jamaica rum,
>   1 slice of lemon.

Grate a little nutmeg on top, and serve.

36. The Old Style of Blue Blazer.

The same as a hot Scotch, only take a hot silver mug, pour in your hot Scotch and light it; leave it burning for about 2 minutes, while you pour it into another hot mug, and *vice versa;* then serve.

37. Hot Brandy.

A hot glass with 2 lumps of sugar, well dissolved in ½ glass of boiling water,

⅔ of brandy,
⅓ of Burgundy.

Mix this well, and add a slice of orange.

38. Hong Kong Punch.

The juice of a lime, and 3 dashes of pineapple-juice in the bottom of a hot, thin glass,

a spoonful of sugar,
a cup of strong boiling tea,
a drink of Jamaica rum,
2 dashes of brandy,
a piece of sliced lemon.

If not hot enough add a little hot water. (You may add a dash of maraschino.)

39. Lait de Poule.

(FOR THE SICK.)

Break the yolks of 2 fresh eggs in the bottom of a glass, beat this up well with a spoonful of sugar, and 3 spoonfuls of orange-flower extract, until the eggs begin to look white; while you stir with one hand, add a glass of hot water, a pony of brandy, and stir well before serving.

40. Hot Italian Lemonade.

The juice of half a lemon and of half an orange,
a large spoonful of sugar.

Fill your glass nearly up with boiling water; add a little Chianti; stir, and serve with a little nutmeg on top.

41. Ladies' Hot Punch.

A hot glass half full of boiling water, with 2 lumps of sugar well dissolved,

½ drink of sherry wine,
½ drink of port wine; mix this well;
1 slice of orange, and a little nutmeg on the top.

42. Hot Orange Lemonade, with Brandy.

In a large wineglass squeeze the juice of a lime, and the juice of an orange,

a large spoonful of sugar; dissolve this well;
1 pony of brandy; mix well.

While you stir with one hand, fill your glass with boiling milk slowly.

43. Hot Red Wine Punch.

A large, hot glass with the juice of half a lemon in the bottom,

3 lumps of sugar,
½ glass of boiling water; dissolve this well;
a glass of claret,
a dash of Jamaica rum.

Mix this thoroughly; add a slice of an orange, and a little cinnamon.

44. Hot Scotch.

A hot glass half full of boiling water,

a lump or two of sugar; dissolve well;
a drink of Scotch whiskey; mix this.

If desired, a little lemon-peel, and a little nutmeg.

45. A Sure Relief.

A punch-glass half full of boiling water,
            2 lumps of sugar; dissolve well;
            1 pony of peppermint,
            1 dash of Jamaica ginger,
            1 pony of brandy,
            1 dash of raspberry syrup,
            the peel of a little lemon, and serve.

46. Black Rose.

A hot glass with 2 lumps of sugar,
            3 or 4 cloves,
            a piece of cinnamon,
            ½ glass of boiling water; mix well.
Fill your glass with Assmannshäuser, and add a piece of
orange.

47. Scotch Delight.

A hot glass with 2 lumps of sugar,
            ½ glass of boiling water; dissolve well;
            ½ of Scotch whiskey,
            ½ of Irish whiskey,
            1 dash of claret.
Mix well, and add a little lemon-peel.

48. Fancy Hot Sherry.

A hot glass half full of boiling water,
            2 small lumps of sugar; dissolve well;
            a drink of sherry,
            a dash of port wine,
            ½ slice of lemon,
            a little cinnamon on the top.

49. Swedish Punch.

A hot glass half filled with boiling water; add to this enough Swedish punch essence to make it palatable; add a little nutmeg if desired.

50. Hot Spiced Rum.

A hot, thin glass half filled with boiling water,

> 1 or 2 lumps of sugar; dissolve this well;
> a drink of Jamaica rum,
> a dash of claret,
> a small piece of butter,
> a roasted cracker,
> 2 or 3 cloves, and serve.

51. Base-Ball Lemonade.

A fresh egg in the bottom of a glass,

> the juice of a lemon,
> a spoonful of sugar,
> a little fine ice,
> ⅓ of water,
> ⅔ of milk.

Shake this very well, and serve.

52. Bavaroise à l'Eau.

A large bar-glass,

> ⅓ full of capillaire syrup,
> 1 barspoonful of orange-flower water.

Fill the glass with boiling water or tea, squeeze the oil of a little lemon-peel on the top.

53. Bavaroise Mexicaine.

Put 1 barspoonful of pulverized sugar and the yolk of an egg in a large glass; stir it well with a spoon,

> 1 pony of old Jamaica rum.

Fill the balance with boiling milk while stirring.

54. Italian Lemonade.

The juice of half a peeled lemon and orange,
a large spoonful of fine sugar,
the glass full of ice.

Fill your glass with water, shake this well, add a little dash of Chianti; ornament with fruits and ice-cream.

55. Raspberry Lemonade, with Wine.

The juice of a lime or a lemon,
a spoonful of sugar,
the juice of 1 dozen raspberries.

Fill your glass with ice, add a glass of sherry or port wine, fill your glass up with water, shake well, ornament with fruits and ice-cream, and serve with a straw.

56. Soda Lemonade.

The juice of ½ lemon,
1 spoonful of sugar,
dissolve well in a large glass,
2 or 3 lumps of ice.

Pour in your plain soda with the left hand while you stir with the right, and serve.

57. Seltzer Lemonade.

It is made the same way, only use Seltzer instead of soda.

58. Strawberry Lemonade.

The juice of a lemon,
1 spoonful of sugar in a large glass.
the juice of 1 dozen strawberries.

Fill your glass one-third full of ice and the balance with milk; shake this very well and strain into a long, thin glass.

59. Violet Lemonade.

Mix a tablespoonful of violet syrup and a spoonful of sugar with the juice of ½ lemon in a glass of water (cold); this is a very pleasant drink, especially adapted against headache and nervous diseases.

60. Another.

In a large glass the juice of half a lemon,
a spoonful of pineapple syrup,
a spoonful of sugar,
3 dashes of crême de violet.
Fill your glass with ice, shake well, ornament with ice-cream and berries, and serve with a straw.

61. Lemonade Parfait.

Put the rind of twelve peeled lemons in three quarts of boiling water; press their juice, after cooling, into the fluid; add one and a half pounds of pulverized sugar, three-fourths of a quart of Rhine wine and 1 pint of boiled milk; stir well and strain through canton flannel.

62. Apricot Sherbet.

From three pounds of ripe apricots select the largest ones, put the smaller ones with three gills of water in a stone pot, let boil until the pits fall out, strain the juice through canton flannel and squeeze the fruits well; boil the juice with one pound of sugar to a thick syrup; boil the larger ones soft in one and a half quarts of water until they burst. Take them out and remove the pits. Strain the water, in which they were boiled, into a bowl, add the syrup, put the fruit in, cut in two, with some lumps of ice, and season with almond essence.

63. Bavaroise au Chocolat.

Put in a vessel partly filled with boiling water a pot with one
quart of milk; break five ounces of vanilla chocolate and drop
it into the milk; stir continually, but never let the milk boil;
hand out the glasses, put in every one a tablespoonful of sugar
syrup and fill in the chocolate concoction; serve it hot

64. Bavaroise à l'Italienne.

Put two teaspoonfuls of pulverized sugar and a bit of powdered
cinnamon in a glass; add one-half of coffee and the other half of
chocolate dissolved in boiling water; serve it hot.

65. Bavaroise au Lait.

Take a large glass, fill it to one-third with capillaire syrup,
add a teaspoonful of orange-flower water and fill it up with boiling milk.

66. Bilberry Lemonade.

One pint of bilberry-juice is mixed with two quarts of cold
water; add one and a half pounds of powdered sugar, in case the
juice should not have been sweetened before; mix well and serve
cold.

67. Cherry Lemonade.

Put two pounds of sour cherries in a tureen, mash them with
a wooden spoon and pour two and a half or three quarts of boiling water over it.   A small portion of the pits is cracked, put
them in the tureen, cover well and let soak about three hours;
filter; mix with a quart of sugar refined and cleared to syrup and
let it get cold.   A spoonful of St. Croix rum or arrack increases
the fine taste of this lemonade exceedingly.

68. Cherry Lemonade.

(FOR THE SICK.)

Mash one pound of dried sour cherries, pits and all, and boil it in one quart of water with the rind of half a lemon and a small stick of cinnamon slowly half an hour; strain through flannel, sweeten with sugar to taste and keep it in a bottle for use.

69. Cherry Sherbet.

From three pounds of sour cherries a number of the largest and finest are selected; the juice of the rest is pressed through a cloth into a pot and heated to boiling with one pound of sugar; the selected large cherries are boiled soft in one to one and a half quarts of water; take them from the fire, lift them out carefully, put them in a bowl with one quart of the water in which they were boiled and with their juice, add a few drops of rose or orange-flower essence and a few lumps of ice, and serve.

70. Citronelle.

Use a large glass with some fine ice,
⅓ glass of green tea,
⅓ glass of black tea,
⅓ glass of lemon syrup.
Shake well, and serve.

71. Currant Lemonade.

Half a quart of fresh currant-juice is mixed with one quart of cold water and one pound of sugar and strained through a flannel; or you take currant syrup; mix one pound of it with the juice of a lemon and one and one-fourth quarts of cold water.

72. English Milk Lemonade.

Peel the rind of two fine lemons very thinly, squeeze the juice of the lemons, cut the rind into small pieces, and let it soak for about twelve hours; filter; mix with two pounds of sugar refined to syrup, a bottle of sherry, and two and a half quarts of fresh, boiling milk. Clear the lemonade by filtering often enough through a flannel bag, and a very cooling summer-drink will crown your efforts.

73. Fig Sherbet.

Cut off the stems of two pounds of large dried figs; pierce each with a wooden pick several times; infuse with one and a half quarts of boiling water over night, strain, add a few drops of orange-flower water, some lumps of ice, and the figs, and serve.

74. Gooseberry Lemonade.

To one quart of water add one pint of gooseberry-juice, and one pound of pulverized sugar.

75. Ice Lemonade.

Well-prepared orange or raspberry lemonade is filled into a bottle; dig this into cracked ice, and serve after three-quarters of an hour, when little lumps of ice are forming in the lemonade.

76. Imperial.

Place in a large, well-warmed pot, one ounce of cremor tartari, the rind of three very thinly peeled lemons, one and a half pounds of sugar; pour over it two and a half quarts of boiling water, cover the pot well, and let it stand an hour in a temperate place; stir now and then; put it on ice, and decant it very carefully.

77. Boiled Lemonade.

Put the rind of two thinly peeled lemons in a tea-pot; then remove the white skin of the fruit, cut them into very thin slices, remove the seeds; put the slices likewise in the pot, and add one pint of boiling water; cover the pot well and let it soak for about ten minutes; drink it hot after sweetening with sugar to taste.

(This lemonade can be very warmly recommended in cases of cold, before going to bed.)

78. Lemonade Gazeuse.

Half an ounce of carbonate of magnesia is ground in one pint of water; fill the milky fluid into a glass bottle, add half an ounce of crystallized citric acid, and close the bottle air-tight. After twelve hours filter the fluid into another bottle, in which you first place one-fourth ounce of citric acid and two ounces of sugar syrup; fill the bottle up with fresh water; cork well; fasten the cork with twine, and shake in order to mix the syrup with the water, and to dissolve the citric acid, which then sets free the carbonic acid in the carbonate of magnesia; which acid makes the lemonade sparkle.

79. Orange Lemonade.

Take one quart of cold water, the juice of three oranges; rub the peel of them slightly on sugar, add a glass of Rhine wine, and sweeten at your discretion.

80. Orange Sherbet.

Six ripe, sweet oranges are peeled; four of them cut in pieces and freed from their white skin and seeds, the other two well squeezed.

Stir this with one-fourth pound of sugar over a slow fire to boiling; let it get cool, thin with fresh water, and add the orange pieces, some drops of orange-flower essence, and a few lumps of ice.

81. Turkish Orange Sherbet.

Peel five or six sweet oranges very carefully, divide them into pieces, cut each piece again in two, remove the seeds and the thin skin; put all in a tureen, then place one-fourth pound of powdered sugar and the juice of two oranges in an enameled pot; stir over a slow fire until it begins to boil; take it from the fire, let it get cool, pour it into the tureen, add one quart of cold water, a few drops of orange-flower essence, a few lumps of ice, stir well and serve.

82. Pear Sherbet.

One or two pounds of dried pears are washed, cut in quarters, freed from seeds and pips, infused in one and a half quarts of boiling water in a well-covered tureen over night; the following day add some sugar, stick cinnamon and lemon-peel; boil until the pears are soft, take them out, strain after cooling, add the pears and some lumps of ice, and serve.

(In the same way it may be prepared from fresh pears.)

83. Persian Sherbet.

One pound of ripe, fresh strawberries are mashed in a tureen with a wooden spoon; add a lemon cut in pieces without the seeds, and a teaspoonful of orange-flower water; pour over it one and a fourth quarts of fresh water, let it stand covered three hours.

Strain through canton flannel, press the fruit hard to make them yield as much juice as possible, add one pound of lump-sugar, stir until the sugar is dissolved, put on ice, and serve.

84. Pomegranate Sherbet.

A few ripe pomegranates are cut in pieces; leave some aside, press the rest through a cloth and boil the juice with the same quantity of water and one-fourth pound of sugar, while continually stirring; boil it·to a thick syrup.

After it is cool pour it into a tureen, add some fresh water, a few drops of orange-flower water, a few lumps of ice and the fruits you left aside.

85. Turkish Raisin Sherbet.

Boil one pound of fine raisins slowly in one pint of water, until they look like the fresh fruit; filter the fluid, and boil this with one-half pound of sugar to a thick syrup; skim well; let it get cool; pour into a glass bowl; diminish too great a sweetness by adding cold water; put the boiled raisins in, a few drops of orange-flower extract, a few lumps of ice, and serve the sherbet in glasses.

86. Raspberry Lemonade.

Press any quantity of fresh raspberries; add to one quart of juice two quarts of fresh water, the juice of a lemon, and half a pound of powdered sugar; strain, and serve in glasses; or you may bottle it, to keep it for a short while.

87. Rhubarb Sherbet.

Boil as much cut rhubarb as is required for filling half a pint in one quart of water with four ounces of sugar, on which the rind of a small lemon has been rubbed off, for half an hour; strain the water, let the sherbet get cold, add some lumps of ice, and serve this very refreshing drink in glasses.

88. Rose-Hip Lemonade.

Very ripe rose-hips are gathered in the latter part of fall, after the first frost; remove the pits, and let the hips dry in the open air in the sun; for each pint of the dried fruit take two quarts of water; boil both together for half an hour; filter through canton flannel, sweeten to taste with sugar, and serve.

89. Wine Lemonade.

Rub the rind of one and a half lemons on one and a half pounds of loaf-sugar; put it in one quart of cold water and one quart of Rhine wine; add the juice of three lemons; mix well, if desired, with some cracked ice, and serve.

90. Wine Sherbet.

Very ripe raspberries, strawberries, cherries, apricots or peaches, are mashed and infused with water for a few hours; press through a clean cloth; mix the juice with two bottles of white wine, the juice of two lemons, and sugar to taste; place it on ice; after cooling, serve.

91. Catawba Cobbler.

A large, long glass,

        a squirt of Seltzer,

        a barspoonful of sugar; mix this well;

        a wineglassful of Catawba wine; mix this;

        fill your glass with shaved ice to the top,

        1 dash of port wine.

Ornament with fruits in season.

If you like, put a spoonful of ice-cream on the top, to make it attractive; serve with a straw and a spoon.

92. Champagne Cobbler.

A delicate wineglass,

        a small lump of sugar,

        fill your glass with shaved ice,

        fill the intervals with champagne.

Stir this in a slow manner; add a little vanilla or strawberry ice-cream, with a nice berry in season, and serve with a straw and a spoon. You may add a little maraschino.

93. Sherry Cobbler.

A fine, large glass,

        a spoonful of sugar,

        1 dash of mineral water; mix this;

        a glass of sherry wine; mix this;

        fill your glass with fine ice,

        a dash of port wine.

Ornament with fruits in season, and ice-cream, and serve with a straw and spoon.

94. Claret Cobbler.

A large, fine glass,
>   a squirt of Seltzer,
>   a spoonful of sugar; mix this;
>   a glass of claret; stir this well;
>   fill your glass with fine ice.

Ornament with fruits and ice-cream, and serve with a straw and spoon.

You may add a dash of Jamaica rum before ornamenting.

(These recipes will do for any cobbler you want.)

95. Plain Gin Fizz.

A large mixing-glass,
>   the juice of half a lemon or lime,
>   ½ spoonful of sugar,
>   ⅔ glassful of fine ice,
>   a drink of Old Tom or Holland gin.

Shake this exceedingly well; strain into a fizz glass; fill the balance with Seltzer, and see that your guest drinks it at once.

96. Silver Fizz.

It is made in the same way as a plain gin fizz, only begin with the white of an egg in the bottom.

97. Golden Fizz.

It is made the same way as the silver fizz, only begin with the yolk of the egg.

98. Royal Fizz.

It is made the same way as the silver fizz, only begin with the whole of an egg.

99. Grand Royal Fizz.

It is made the same way as the royal fizz, only add a little orange-juice, a dash of maraschino and a dash of parfait amour or crême de roses.

100. Imperial Fizz.

This drink may be prepared, although it is made essentially the same way as the grand royal fizz, out of almost any kind of liquor—such as gin, whiskey or brandy; add, instead of Seltzer or mineral water, champagne. This drink is intended for a company of from three to six persons.

101. Cream Fizz.

This is made the same way as other fizzes, only put a small portion of cream in your glass before shaking; then put in the Seltzer; use a glass a little larger.

102. Violet Fizz.

The juice of half a lemon and half a lime,
>a little sugar in the bottom of a glass,
>⅔ glassful of fine ice,
>1 drink of Old Tom gin,
>2 dashes of genuine raspberry syrup,
>a pony of cream.

Shake it up quickly, strain into a fizz glass, add a little Seltzer, and serve.

You may use Holland gin instead of Old Tom.

103. Sitting Bull Fizz.

A glass of cracked ice,
>the juice of a large lemon,
>a spoonful of fine sugar,
>⅓ drink of Santa Cruz rum,
>⅔ drink of whiskey.

Shake to the freezing-point, strain into a fizz glass and fill the balance with Seltzer.

104. Absinthe Frappé.

(AMERICAN STYLE.)

A mixing-glass with fine ice,
    1 dash of gum,
    1 ½ ponies of absinthe.

Shake this exceedingly well, strain into a cocktail glass, and serve.

105. Absinthe à la Parisienne.

A medium-sized glass,
    a drink of absinthe in the bottom.

Fill your glass with cold water, by letting it drip into the glass very slowly.

106. Absinthe aux Dieux

A tumbler ⅔ full of ice,
    2 dashes of gum,
    1 pony of absinthe,
    1 dash of maraschino.

Shake it heartily; freeze to the coldest degree; strain into a cocktail glass; drop a little crême de roses in the centre, and serve.

107. The Great Admiral.

(FOR TWO.)

A mixing-tumbler,
    the juice of a peeled orange,
    4 dashes of gum,
    ⅔ glass of fine ice,
    2 dashes of curaçao,
    1 drink of brandy,
    ½ drink of Jamaica rum,
    2 dashes of crême de cocoa,
    1 dash of anisette,
    1 dash of crême de roses.

Mix this very well; strain into fancy glasses, and serve.

108. Alabazam.

A large barglass,

the juice of ½ lemon,
1 barspoonful of sugar,
1 dash of Seltzer; mix this well;
fill your glass ⅔ with fine ice,
2 dashes of curaçao,
1 drink of brandy.

Stir well, strain, and serve.

109. L'Appetit.

A whiskey-glass,

2 lumps of ice,
⅔ of vino vermouth,
⅓ of Fernet branca,
1 slice of orange.

This drink is much *en vogue* among southern Europeans.

110. Apple Blossom.

A glass with ice,

4 dashes of gum,
a small drink of apple-jack,
2 dashes of crême de roses.

Freeze this thoroughly; strain, and serve.

111. Après Souper.

(FOR TWO.)

A mixing-glass filled with shaved ice,

2 dashes of gum,
1 pony of crême de menthe,
½ pony of maraschino,
1 small drink of brandy.

Stir this, strain and serve.

112. Avant Souper.

A whiskey-tumbler with 2 lumps of ice,
2 drops of gum,
1 pony of absinthe.

Let it stand for about two minutes.   Fill your glass up with
water slowly, by letting the water drip; remove the ice, and serve.

113. Avant Déjeuner.

A large glass with a good portion of imported Seltzer,
a spoonful of sugar; mix this;
a glass of Moselle wine; mix this;
fill up with ice,
1 dash of port wine.

Ornament the top with fruits in season.

114. L'Arc de Triomphe.

Divide a pint of dry champagne frappé in 2 glasses,
1 lump of sugar in each with a spoon,
1 pony of cognac to each glass.

Stir up well before serving.

115. Egg Beer.

Beat a whole egg with a spoonful of sugar in a glass, and fill
it up with beer.

116. A Pansy Blossom.

(FOR TWO.)

A large tumbler with some fine ice,
6 dashes of gum,
¼ glass of Russian kümmel,
¼ glass of absinthe,
¼ glass of vino vermouth,
¼ glass of maraschino,
the whites of two eggs.

Shake to the coldest point; strain into 2 fancy glasses, and
serve.

117. Le Bon Boire.

(FOR FOUR.)

A large glass with ice,

$\frac{1}{10}$ of maraschino,
$\frac{1}{10}$ of anisette,
$\frac{1}{10}$ of crême de roses,
$\frac{1}{10}$ of crême de vanille,
$\frac{1}{10}$ of parfait amour,
$\frac{1}{10}$ of crême dė thé (tea),
$\frac{1}{10}$ of celestine,
$\frac{1}{10}$ of crême de cocoa,
$\frac{1}{10}$ of fine old brandy,
$\frac{1}{10}$ of Benedictine.

Shake well, strain, and serve in fancy glasses.

118. Brahmapootra.

An egg, and a spoonful of sugar in a glass,

a little lemon-juice; fill your glass with ice;
1 pony of brandy,
1 dash of crême de roses,
1 dash of crême de mocha,
1 dash of crême de vanille,
a little cream.

Shake well, strain, and serve.

119. Brandy Crusta.

A mixing-glass,

a little sugar,
a little plain water, enough to dissolve it;
fill the glass $\frac{2}{3}$ full of ice,
stir this well;
a drink of brandy; mix again.

Pare a round, clean lemon; place this on the inside of a wine-glass; strain your mixture into it, and serve.

120. Brandy Rose.

A goblet with fine ice,

2 dashes of curaçao,

2 dashes of parfait amour,

1 dash of maraschino,

½ dash of peppermint cordial,

1 ½ ponies of brandy.

Mix well, and serve.

121. Brandy Toddy.

A mixing-glass,

half a spoonful of sugar,

a little water, enough to dissolve the sugar,

⅔ full of ice,

1 drink of brandy.

Stir this very well; strain into a cocktail glass; grate a little nutmeg on top.

(Any other toddy may be prepared the same way.)

122. The Bridge Bracer.

A large glass with fine ice,

beat a fresh egg,

1 barspoonful of powdered sugar,

2 dashes of bitters,

1 pony of brandy.

Mix this; add a bottle of imported ginger ale; stir thoroughly, strain, and serve.

123. The Broker's Thought.

The white of an egg in a mixing-glass,

the juice of a lime,

a little fine sugar,

some fine ice,

⅔ drink of whiskey,

⅓ drink of Santa Cruz rum.

Shake this thoroughly well; strain into a fancy glass; fill up with milk, while you stir it with a spoon, and serve.

124. The Lily Bouquet.

(FOR TWO.)

A goblet with fine ice,

3 dashes of gum,

2 ponies of absinthe,

2 ponies of benedictine,

2 dashes of crême de roses,

1 dash of anisette,

the whites of two eggs.

Shake very well, strain, and serve.

125. Calla Lily.

(FOR TWO.)

In a mixing-glass put the yolks of 2 fresh eggs,

a spoonful of sugar,

½ glassful of fine ice,

1½ ponies of brandy,

1½ ponies of Jamaica rum,

1 dash of maraschino,

2 ponies of cream,

a few drops of crême de roses;

shake this well.

Whip the whites of the eggs into a snowy foam with a little sugar. Pour out your drink into two glasses, and crown the whole with the foam.

126. Claret Punch.

A large, thin glass,

the juice of half a lemon,

a squirt of Seltzer,

a spoonful of sugar; mix well;

a glass of claret; mix this again.

Fill your glass with fine ice to the top; put some ice-cream on top; ornament with orange and berries in season.

127. Chocolate Punch.

A glass with an egg in the bottom,

a spoonful of sugar,
⅔ of brandy,
⅓ of port wine,
1 dash of crême de cocoa,
1 pony of cream.

Fill your glass with ice; shake well; strain, and serve.

128. Claret Cup.

A good sized bowl,

½ pony of maraschino,
½ pony of curaçao,
½ pony of benedictine,
½ pony of chartreuse (yellow),
the juice of 6 limes,
2 bottles of claret,
1 bottle of Rhine wine or Moselle,
a bottle of Apollinaris,
½ pound of sugar,
a little rind of a cucumber,
a little orange and pineapple sliced,
a few sprigs of mint.

Stir this very well; add a little coarse ice, and serve.

129. The Cosmopolitan Cooler.

A long glass,

the juice of 2 limes,
a few dashes of Seltzer,
a spoonful of powdered sugar,
mix this well;
a drink of Santa Cruz rum,
then fill the glass with fine ice,
stir all ingredients well;
a dash of Jamaica rum.

Crown it with vanilla ice-cream and ornament with berries lightly powdered with sugar; serve with a straw.

130. Champagne Cup.

It is made like a claret cup, only use champagne instead of claret.

131. Columbus Punch.

The juice of half an orange and the juice of half a lemon in the bottom of the glass; dissolve this with a spoonful of sugar and a dash of mineral water,

> 1 glass of Chianti,
> 2 dashes of Jamaica rum,
> 1 dash of maraschino,
> 1 dash of brandy.

Mix this well, fill your glass with fine ice, add a dash of Rosoglio and ornament with fruits and ice-cream.

132. Coffee and Rum.

(FOR COLD AND SORE THROAT.)

Break an egg in a glass, beat it up well;

> a spoonful of sugar,
> a drink of old Jamaica rum.

Mix this up well, pour in a cup of the best mocha or Java coffee—hot—and finish with a piece of best butter. Best take this drink right after rising.

133. The Correspondent.

A pony glass,

> ⅓ of crême de roses,
> ⅓ of green chartreuse,
> ⅓ of brandy.

Light this for two minutes and serve.

134. Easter Crocus.

A large mixing-tumbler,
a fresh egg in its bottom,
the juice of ½ a lemon,
1 barspoonful of sugar,
fill the tumbler with ice,
1 drink of Old Tom gin,
1 dash of maraschino,
1 dash of crême de vanille.

Shake this thoroughly well; pour out into a thin glass and fill the little vacant space with ginger ale.

135. The Southern Cross.

A mixing-glass,
the juice of a lime,
a dash of mineral water,
a spoonful of sugar,
⅔ of St. Croix rum,
⅓ of brandy,
1 dash of curaçao.

Stir this well, fill your glass with fine ice, stir again and strain into a sour glass.

136. The Crown.

A pony glass,
⅓ of maraschino,
⅓ of green chartreuse,
⅓ of benedictine, each separate.

137. Curaçao Punch.

A long, thin glass,
the juice of half a lemon,
4 dashes of gum,
½ pony of brandy,
½ pony of Jamaica rum,
½ pony of curaçao.

Fill your glass with ice, stir well, ornament with fruits and ice-cream, serve with a spoon and straw.

138. "The World's" Morning Delight.

A large tumbler,
>the juice of half a lemon,
>the juice of half an orange,
>a little fine sugar,
>2 dashes of Russian kümmel,
>2 dashes of maraschino,
>1½ ponies of absinthe.

Fill your glass with fine ice, shake this well, strain, add some Seltzer and serve.

139. Ladies' Delight.

A large, thin glass,
>a spoonful of sugar,
>a cup of cold coffee,
>⅔ of brandy,
>⅓ of Jamaica rum.

Fill your glass with ice, stir well, ornament with ice-cream and berries, and serve with spoon and a straw.

140. The Duplex.

(FOR TWO.)

Break 2 eggs in a large glass,
>2 barspoonfuls of powdered sugar,
>⅔ full of ice,
>1 drink of sherry,
>1 drink of port wine,
>½ pony of benedictine,
>a small whiskey tumbler of cream.

Shake extremely well and strain into two fine glasses.

141. General Harrison's Egg-Nogg.

It is made as any egg-nogg, only use cider instead of liquor, and no milk.

142. Egg-Nogg.

A large mixing-glass,
> a fresh egg in its bottom,
> a tablespoonful of sugar,
> a little fine ice,
> ⅓ of Santa Cruz rum,
> ⅔ of brandy,
> 1 dash of maraschino or crême de vanille.

Fill your glass with milk; shake this exceedingly well, strain into a large, thin glass, add the oil of a little lemon-peel on the top, and serve.

(This drink may be made of almost any kind of liquor that is desired.)

143. Eye-Opener.

The juice of ½ a lime in a glass,
> a spoonful of sugar,
> the white of an egg,
> a little drink of Irish whiskey,
> 2 dashes of Tonic Phospate,
> ⅔ full of ice.

Shake, strain and fill balance with Seltzer.

144. The Foundation.

(FOR TWO.)

A large tumbler with 2 fresh eggs,
> the juice of a lemon,
> 2 barspoonfuls of sugar,
> ½ glass of shaved ice,
> 2 dashes of calisaya,
> 2 drinks of Old Tom gin,
> 1 dash of absinthe,
> 2 dashes of vino vermouth.

Shake for full 2 minutes; strain into a high glass; fill the balance with carbonic water, and serve.

145. Encore.

A pony glass,
>> ⅓ of maraschino,
>> ⅓ of curaçao,
>> ⅓ of brandy; each separate.

Light it and serve.

146. Sherry Filler.

The yolk of an egg in a mixing-glass,
>> a spoonful of sugar,
>> a drink of sherry wine,
>> 1 dash of crême de roses,
>> ⅔ full of ice.

Shake this well, and serve.

147. Le Fin du Siècle.

(WILLIAM'S PRIDE.)

A mixing-glass with the juice of half an orange,
>> the juice of ¼ of a lemon,
>> ½ spoonful of sugar,
>> the yolk of an egg,
>> ½ pony of brandy,
>> ½ pony of benedictine,
>> ½ pony of maraschino,
>> 1 dash of curaçao,
>> 1 dash of anisette,
>> 1 dash of parfait amour,
>> 1 dash of noyeau,
>> 3 ponies of pure cream.

Fill your glass with fine ice, shake it extra well; strain into a fancy glass; ornament the top with the white of an egg, that you have beaten up to the form of frozen snow, and sweetened with sugar; serve with a spoon.

148. Lafayette Flip.

Drop into a large glass a fresh egg,

        1 barspoonful of powdered sugar,
        1 pony of old Rye whiskey,
        a dash of green chartreuse,
        2 dashes of curaçao,
        2 ponies of cream,
        a few lumps of ice.

Shake this all well, and strain into a fancy glass.

149. Sherry Flip.

(FOR TWO.)

Into a large glass 2 eggs,

        2 spoonfuls of sugar,
        ¼ glass of fine ice,
        2 glasses of sherry wine,
        1 small glass of cream.

Shake this exceedingly well, and serve. You may add a dash of maraschino.

150. Forget-Me-Not.

A mixing-glass with ice,

        the juice of a lime,
        a spoonful of sugar,
        a drink of brandy,
        a dash of maraschino,
        the white of an egg.

Shake this well, strain and serve.

151. Frappé à la Guillaume.

2 dashes of gum in the bottom of the glass,

        fill your glass with ice,
        1 pony of absinthe,
        ½ pony of vino vermouth,
        2 dashes of anisette.

Freeze this to the coldest point, and serve.

152. The Mayflower.

(FOR TWO.)

A glass with ice,

6 dashes of gum,
¼ of Russian kümmel,
¼ of brandy,
¼ of vino vermouth,
¼ of crême de cocoa,
1 dash of parfait amour,
the yolks of two eggs.

Shake well, strain and serve.

153. Fruit Frappé.

Into a mixing-tumbler the juice of half a lemon,

a little orange-juice,
1 barspoonful of sugar,
2 barspoonfuls of pineapple syrup,
1 pony of rich cream,
a drink of Santa Cruz rum.

Pack your goblet with fine ice, and shake to the freezing-point; strain into a fancy glass, and serve.

154. Whiskey Frappé.

A large glass with ice,

2 dashes of gum,
a drink of whiskey.

Shake for 2 minutes, and serve.

155. The Judge.

A mixing-glass ⅔ full of ice,

3 dashes of gum,
⅓ of crême de menthe,
⅔ of brandy.

Shake to the freezing-point; strain, and serve in a cocktail glass.

156. Porter Flip.

A long, thin glass with an egg in the bottom,
a spoonful of sugar,
fill your glass with porter,
stir very well.
A little nutmeg on top, and the oil of a little lemon-peel.

157. The Gem.

A mixing-glass,
the juice of a lime,
a little pineapple syrup,
a spoonful of sugar; dissolve well;
½ drink of Santa Cruz rum,
½ drink of brandy.
Mix this well, fill your glass with ice, and mix again; strain into a fine glass; place a slice of lemon on the top, and grate a little cinnamon upon it.

158. Genuine Whiskey Punch.

A goblet filled with fine ice,
a dash of lemon-juice,
3 dashes of gum,
1 drink of whiskey.
Then fill another goblet with fine ice, and put this on top of the first; turn them upside down five or six times; hold them up together as high as you can with both hands, and let the liquid drip down into a tall, fancy glass; 1 dash of Jamaica rum on the top, and you will have an impressive and pleasant drink.

(Other liquors may be turned into punches the same way.)

159. Gin Puff.

A large glass with a drink of gin; fill your glass half with milk and the balance with Seltzer, while you stir it.

160. Gilmore Punch.

The juice of a lime in a fine, tall glass,
>   the juice of half an orange,
>   a small spoonful of sugar; mix this;
>   fill the glass with cracked ice,
>   1 dash of maraschino,
>   1 dash of curaçao,
>   1 dash of green chartreuse,
>   1 dash of benedictine,
>   1 drink of Irish whiskey.

Stir well, and ornament with vanilla ice-cream and fruits in season.

161. The Glorious Fourth.

A glass with the juice of a lime,
>   4 dashes of gum,
>   ⅔ full of ice,
>   1 drink of brandy,
>   1 dash of Jamaica rum,
>   a large tablespoonful of ice-cream.

Shake this exceedingly well; strain into a fancy glass, and serve.

162. Hannibal Hamlin.

A mixing-tumbler,
>   the juice of half a lemon,
>   the juice of half an orange,
>   fill it with cracked ice,
>   ⅔ of peach brandy,
>   ⅓ of old Jamaica rum,
>   2 tablespoonfuls of honey.

Shake to the freezing-point, and strain into a fancy glass.

163. Happy Moment.

A pony glass,
>   ⅓ of crême de roses,
>   ⅓ of maraschino,
>   ⅓ of benedictine,
>   1 drop of bitters in the centre.

164. Heart's Content.

(FOR TWO.)

A mixing-glass with ⅔ of fine ice,

    1 pony of brandy,
    1 pony of benedictine,
    1 pony of maraschino,
    1 pony of parfait amour.

Shake this thoroughly; strain into fine wineglasses; beat up the white of an egg to the form of frozen snow with a little sugar; put this on top of your drink; squeeze a little lemon-peel on it, and serve with a spoon.

165. My Hope.

A whiskey glass with 2 dashes of gum,

    1 dash of bitters,
    ⅔ of brandy,
    ⅓ of port wine,
    a little red pepper.

Stir this well, and serve.

166. The Invitation.

(FOR TWO.)

A glass with 2 dashes of gum,

    some fine ice,
    1 small drink of sherry wine,
    1 small drink of vino vermouth,
    2 dashes of absinthe.

Freeze this to the coldest point; strain into 2 fancy glasses, and serve.

167. Jamaica Rum à la Créole.

The juice of half a lime,

    a dash of Seltzer,
    1 spoonful of sugar; dissolve this;
    a drink of Jamaica rum; mix this;
    fill your glass with ice,
    a dash of port wine.

Ornament with fruits and ice-cream.

168. John Collins.

A large glass with the juice of half a lemon,
          a spoonful of sugar,
          a full drink of Holland gin.
Mix this well; add two or three lumps of ice; fill your glass
up with Seltzer, while you stir.

169. The Kaleidoscope.

A mixing-glass with some cracked ice,
          1 pony of absinthe,
          1 pony of vino vermouth,
          3 dashes of maraschino,
          3 dashes of benedictine,
          3 dashes of curaçao,
          3 dashes of crême de cocoa.
Shake to the freezing-point; strain into a fine wineglass, and
serve.

170. The Knickerbocker.

The juice of half a lime or lemon in a glass,
          3 dashes of raspberry syrup,
          1 wineglassful of Jamaica rum,
          1 dash of curaçao,
          a little cracked ice.
Stir this well; strain, and serve in a fancy glass.

171. The Ladies' Great Favorite.

A large glass,
          a squirt of Seltzer,
          a spoonful of fine sugar,
          fill a wineglass half full with sherry and
          the other half with port wine,
          1 dash of brandy;
          mix this well.
Fill your glass with shaved ice; ornament with orange and
pineapple, and top it off with ice-cream; serve with a spoon.

172. Lait de Poule

(FOR LADIES.)

Beat the yolk of an egg with 2 tablespoonfuls of powdered sugar to foam,

a pony of rum, or kirschwasser, etc.

Stir continually while filling the glass with hot milk, and serve.

173. A Maiden's Kiss.

⅕ of maraschino in a sherry glass,
⅕ of crême de roses,
⅕ of curaçao (white),
⅕ of chartreuse (yellow),
⅕ of benedictine, each separate.

174. The Manhattan Cooler.

A large glass,

the juice of a lime,
a spoonful of sugar; mix this well;
3 or 4 lumps of ice,
1 glass of claret,
1 dash of Santa Cruz rum,
1 bottle of plain soda.

Mix this and serve with a little fruit.

175. The Mayor.

(AN IMITATION OF A MINT JULEP.)

A large glass with an egg in the bottom,

a barspoonful of sugar,
2 dashes of absinthe,
⅓ of vino vermouth,
⅔ of kümmel,
2 gills of cream.

Fill your glass with ice; freeze to the lowest point; strain into a tall glass; squeeze a little lemon-peel on it.

176. Our Milk Punch.

A large glass,

> ⅔ of Santa Cruz rum,
> ⅓ of brandy,
> 1 dash of crême de vanille,
> 1 spoonful of sugar,
> a little fine ice.

Fill your glass with milk, shake thoroughly, strain and serve,

Add a little nutmeg, if you wish, or squeeze a little lemon-peel on it.

177. Strained Mint Julep.

Put the leaves of two sprigs of mint in a mixing-glass with a spoonful of sugar and a little water to dissolve it.

With a squeezing-stick squeeze out the extract of the leaves,

> 1 drink of brandy.

Fill your glass with ice; stir well, strain into a long champagne glass, add a dash of Jamaica rum on the top carefully; place a little sprig of mint on the side of the glass, sprinkle a little sugar on the leaves, and serve.

(You may use other liquors instead of brandy.)

178. Mint Julep.

Use a large, long glass; select three long sprigs of luxuriant mint and let the stems rest on the bottom of the glass. Then take two sprigs of mint, strip them and put the leaves in a mixing-glass; 1 spoonful of sugar, 1 squirt of Seltzer; crush out the extract of the leaves with a squeezing-stick; 1 drink of brandy; stir this and strain into your original glass; fill it with ice and stir; a dash of Jamaica rum on top, ornament the brim of the glass with fruits and the centre with ice-cream and berries. Sprinkle a little sugar over your leaves and serve with a straw.

You may put a little rosebud on your drink.

179. The Ne Plus Ultra.

A sherry glass,

¼ of crême de roses,
¼ of green chartreuse,
¼ of benedictine,
¼ of brandy.

Set fire to the brandy, let burn for two minutes, and serve.

180. The Morning Delight.

In a mixing-glass put the white of an egg,
the juice of a lime,
the juice of half an orange,
fill your glass with ice,
½ pony of absinthe,
1 pony of whiskey,
½ pony of sherry wine,
1 spoonful of sugar,
2 dashes of calisaya.

Shake this well; strain into a fancy glass and fill the balance with seltzer.

181. The Nap.

A cocktail glass filled with ice,

⅓ of kümmel,
⅓ of green chartreuse,
⅓ of brandy.

Drop a dash of crême de roses on top, which will go to the bottom, and serve.

182. New Orleans Punch.

A thin glass with the juice of half a lemon,
1 spoonful of sugar; mix this;
fill with fine ice,
⅔ of St. Julien,
⅓ of Jamaica rum,
1 dash of brandy.

Stir this very well; ornament with fruits in season and a little ice-cream on the top, and serve with a straw.

183. The Opera.

(FOR TWO.)

Break two eggs in the bottom of a mixing-glass,
>   2 barspoonfuls of powdered sugar,
>   2 ponies of fine brandy,
>   fill your glass with cracked ice.

Shake the mixture thoroughly.

A pint bottle of champagne as cold as possible is poured out into two ice-cold glasses with room enough for your first mixture, which is to be strained into the cold champagne very slowly; care must be taken not to have the mixture overflow.

184. Orange County Pride.

A goblet with the juice of a lime,
>   a squirt of Seltzer,
>   a spoonful of sugar; dissolve this well·
>   1 drink of apple-jack.

Fill your glass with ice to the top and stir.   Add a dash of dark-colored brandy; ornament with fruits and serve with a straw.

185. Orange County Punch.

A mixing-glass with a fresh egg in the bottom,
>   the juice of a lemon,
>   1 barspoonful of powdered sugar,
>   a glass of fine apple cider,
>   fill with ice.

Shake thoroughly, strain, and fill up with Seltzer.

186. Palate Tickler.

(FOR COLD.)

A little lemon-juice in a tumbler with some genuine New Orleans molasses,
>   a drink of old Jamaica rum,

Stir exceedingly well, and serve,

187. The "New York Herald."

(FOR TWO.)

A large mixing-glass with the yolks of two eggs in the bottom,
the juice of an orange,
a little pineapple juice,
1 barspoonful of sugar,
1 drink of fine brandy,
1 pony of kirschwasser,
½ pony of curaçao,
½ pony of maraschino,
½ pony of crême de roses,
2 dashes of benedictine,
2 dashes of crême de cocoa.

Fill your glass with fine ice; a large claret glass with pure
cream; shake this exceedingly well; strain into two fancy glasses
so as to fill them.   Beat up the white of one egg to the form of
frozen snow; sweeten this well with sugar; put this on the top of
your drinks; squeeze a little lemon-peel on each, and serve with
a spoon.   This is intended for an evening drink, only on special
occasions.

188. The Paymaster.

A cocktail glass with fine ice,
⅔ of crême de menthe,
⅓ of brandy.

Drop a little bitters in the centre and put a piece of lemon-
peel on the brim of the glass; serve.

189. Peach and Honey.

A whiskey tumbler,
the juice of half a lime or lemon,
a good part of real honey,
a drink of peach brandy.

Stir very well before serving.

(Molasses may be used; also Jamaica rum.)

190. Piazza.

(A VARIATION OF THE OLD FLOSTER.)

A barspoonful of sugar in a large glass,
    a bottle of plain soda,
    2 or 3 lumps of ice,
    a drink of sherry,
    a dash of crême de cocoa.

Mix this thoroughly well, and serve.

This is a drink specially delicious when you are thirsty.

191. Pineapple Julep.

A large glass, with a little pineapple-juice,
    the juice of one-fourth of an orange,
    2 dashes of raspberry syrup,
    2 dashes of maraschino,
    ½ pony of old gin,
    1 glass of champagne or sparkling wine.

Fill your glass with ice, stir this very well, ornament with fruits and ice-cream, and serve with a straw.

192. Pineapple Punch.

A large glass,
    ½ wineglassful of pineapple-juice,
    the juice of half an orange,
    2 dashes of raspberry syrup,
    a little sugar,
    1 dash of maraschino,
    ½ drink of Tom gin,
    ½ drink of Moselle wine.

Stir well; fill your glass with ice; ornament with pineapple and berries, and serve with a straw.

193. The Poem.

A pony glass,
    ⅓ of crême de roses,
    ⅓ of curaçao,
    ⅓ of benedictine, each separate.

194. Porter Sangaree.

A long, thin glass,

      a spoonful of sugar,

      fill your glass with porter.

Stir very well, add a little nutmeg and squeeze a little lemon-peel on top.

195. Port-Wine Sangaree.

A mixing-glass with fine ice,

      3 dashes of gum,

      1 glass of port wine.

Stir this very well, strain into a fine, tall glass, cut a few slices of a peeled lemon, drop them in the drink, grate a little nutmeg on the top and present.

(Other sangarees may be prepared the same way.)

196. The Primrose.

A long, thin glass,

      the juice of half an orange,

      ½ spoonful of sugar,

      1 dash of mineral water,

      1 dash of parfait amour,

      ⅔ of sherry wine,

      ⅓ of port wine.

Mix this well; fill your glass with ice; ornament with fruits and ice-cream.

197. The Press.

The white of an egg in the bottom of a glass,

      3 dashes of lemon-juice,

      1 spoonful of sugar,

      ⅔ of whiskey,

      1 dash of St. Croix rum,

      1 dash of calisaya,

      1 dash of absinthe.

Fill your glass with ice, shake well, strain into a fizz-glass and fill the balance with Seltzer.

198. Pousse l' Amour.

Fill a sherry glass,

⅓ of maraschino,
the yolk of one fresh egg,
⅓ of crême de roses,
⅓ of brandy, each separate.

199. The Promenade.

An egg in the bottom of the glass,

the glass two-thirds full of fine ice,
a barspoonful of fine sugar,
⅔ pony of brandy,
⅓ pony of crême de cocoa,
½ pony of port wine,
2 ponies of cream,

Shake this very well, and strain into a fancy glass.

200. Pousse Café.

A sherry glass,

⅙ of crême de roses, or raspberry syrup,
⅙ of maraschino,
⅙ of curaçao,
⅙ of benedictine,
⅙ of chartreuse (green),
⅙ of brandy, each separate.

You may drop in a little bitters on the top, and set fire to the brandy. While burning, squeeze a little orange-peel on it, which will produce a fine pyrotechnical effect.)

201. The "World's" Pousse Café.

¼ of maraschino,
¼ of crême de roses,
¼ of benedictine,
¼ of brandy, each separate.

A drop of bitters in the centre; set fire to the brandy, and serve.

202. La Première.

(FOR TWO.)

Place the leaves of four sprigs of mint and one-half spoonful of sugar in a large tumbler,

2 dashes of mineral water.

Squeeze out the extract, to give it a dark green tincture. Fill your tumbler two-thirds full of chopped ice; add two small drinks of Tom gin; stir to a very cold degree; strain into two cocktail glasses; place a small sprig of mint in each, allowing the stem to rest on the bottom; sprinkle a little sugar on the leaves; add a little champagne, and serve.

203. The Life-Prolonger.

A large glass, with a fresh egg,

1 spoonful of fine sugar,
⅔ full of fine ice,
⅔ of sherry wine,
⅓ of port wine,
1 dash of crême de roses,
2 ponies of cream.

Shake this exceedingly well, strain into a large glass, and serve.

204. The Queen of Night.

A glass, with a dash of chartreuse in the bottom,

⅔ of port wine,
⅓ of Madeira,
1 dash of brandy,
1 dash of crême de roses,
2 dashes of gum.

Fill your glass with ice; mix well; strain, and serve in a cut glass.

205. The Queen of Sheba.

(FOR TWO.)

A large glass, with the yolks of two eggs,
2 barspoonfuls of sugar,
1 dash of vino vermouth,
1 dash of port wine,
2 dashes of sherry,
1 ½ drinks of brandy,
2 dashes of maraschino,
1 dash of curaçao.

Fill your glass with ice; shake well, strain into two long, thin glasses; crown them with the whites of the two eggs beaten to a hard consistency, and sprinkle colored sugar on the top of it.

206. The Rainbow.

A sherry glass,
⅐ of maraschino,
⅐ of crême de menthe,
⅐ of apricotine,
⅐ of curaçao,
⅐ of yellow chartreuse,
⅐ of green chartreuse,
⅐ of brandy, each separate.

Set fire to the brandy, and serve.

207. The Reliever.

The white of an egg in the bottom of a glass,
the juice of half a lemon,
a barspoonful of sugar,
⅔ glass of fine ice,
⅔ of Jamaica rum,
⅓ of port wine.

Shake this for a full minute; strain into a fancy glass, and serve.

208. The Reminder.

A goblet, with

      1 dash of maraschino,
      1 dash of crême de roses,
      ⅔ glass of fine ice,
      ⅓ of sherry,
      ⅓ of port wine,
      ⅓ of vino vermouth.

Mix this thoroughly; strain into a fancy glass, and serve.

209. Roman Punch.

A large, thin glass,

      the juice of an orange,
      the juice of half a lime or lemon in the bottom,
      a spoonful of sugar,
      a squirt of mineral water,
      dissolve this well;
      ½ pony of curaçao,
      ½ pony of maraschino,
      1 pony of brandy,
      1 dash of Jamaica rum.

Mix this thoroughly well; fill your glass with fine ice; ornament the brim with oranges and pineapple, and the centre with ice-cream and berries. Serve with a spoon and a straw.

210. Reverie.

A mixing-glass, with ice,

      2 dashes of gum,
      1 pony of brandy,
      ½ pony of maraschino,
      ½ pony of curaçao,
      ⅓ glass of vanilla ice-cream.

Shake this very well; strain and serve.

211. The Requiem.

In a mixing-glass an egg,
>> a spoonful of powdered sugar,
>> 1 pony of brandy,
>> 1 dash of sherry,
>> 1 dash of port wine,
>> 1 dash of maraschino,
>> 1 pony of cream.

Fill your glass with ice, shake it and strain into a high champagne glass.

212. Sans Souci.

(FOR TWO.)

A large glass, with the juice of a lime or lemon,
>> a spoonful of sugar,
>> the yolks of two eggs,
>> fill your glass two-thirds full of ice,
>> 2 ponies of absinthe,
>> 1 pony of maraschino,
>> 1 pony of vermouth,
>> 1 dash of white curaçao.

Shake this exceedingly well; strain into two fancy wine-glasses, beat up the white of one egg to the form of frozen snow, with some sugar ; put this on top of your two drinks, and serve with a spoon.

213. The Senator.

A glass with shaved ice,
>> ⅙ of brandy,
>> ⅙ of maraschino,
>> ⅙ of curaçao,
>> ⅙ of chartreuse,
>> ⅙ of benedictine,
>> ⅙ of crême de roses.

Shake this well, strain into a cocktail glass, and serve.

214. The Shandy Gaff.

A glass of Bass ale and a glass of ginger ale are mixed in a glass together, and served.

215. The Snowball.

A large glass with an egg; beat up well with a little powdered sugar, add a bottle of genuine cold ginger ale while you stir it thoroughly, and serve. You may add a pony of brandy.

216. "The Sun."

The juice of half an orange and half a lime in the bottom of a large, thin glass; add and dissolve a spoonful of powdered sugar with a dash of mineral water,

> 1 pony of fine brandy,
> ½ pony of Jamaica rum,
> 1 dash of benedictine,
> 1 dash of curaçao,
> 1 dash of crême de roses.

Mix this thoroughly, fill your glass with fine ice; stir well; ornament with frozen snow in the centre, and the brim with fruits; write on the top of the snow "The Sun," with nutmeg.

Should you have no real snow, beat up the white of an egg with a little fine sugar.

217. "The Evening Sun."

(FOR FOUR.)

In a large glass,

> the juice of a large lemon,
> 2 barspoonfuls of powdered sugar,
> fill the glass with chopped ice,
> a drink of fine brandy,
> a pony of green chartreuse,
> ½ pony of crême de roses,
> the whites of 2 eggs.

Shake this to the freezing-point.

In four glasses divide a pint of dry champagne; strain your ingredients into these four glasses very slowly, and serve.

218. Tansy and Gin.

Place a little tansy in a tumbler, add a little sugar, mix with a little water to extract the substance of the tansy; pour in gin (Holland or Old Tom), and serve with a spoon.

219. Tom and Jerry.

Break the yolks of six eggs in the bottom of a large bowl; beat it long enough to make bubbles appear on the top; stir in some fine sugar gradually, until the mixture becomes hard enough, so that you may take out a spoonful of it without spilling anything; beat the whites of the eggs into the form of frozen snow in another bowl; add one-half of this to your first mixture; mix this together with two ponies of maraschino and two ponies of crême de vanille, take a tablespoonful of this mixture in a fancy Tom-and-Jerry cup; add a small drink of either brandy, whiskey, rum, sherry wine or port wine; mix this well; fill the balance with boiling milk; put a little of the white of the eggs you have got left on the top; add a little ground cinnamon and your drink is ready.

(To keep your mixture in the bowl from getting hard, put a small glass of ale on the top.)

220. Tip-Top Sip.

A goblet with a dash of crême de roses,
> 1 dash of absinthe,
> ⅓ of sherry wine,
> ⅓ of port wine,
> ⅓ of vino vermouth,
> a little fine ice.

Mix this thoroughly, strain into a fancy glass, and present.

221. La Vie Parisienne.

Mix one part of Burgundy and two parts of champagne in your glass.   (This drink is one of the richest.)

Also porter (Dublin Stout) may be mixed the same way with champagne with a most satisfactory result.

222. Tom Collins.

The juice of half a lemon in a large glass,
a barspoonful of sugar,
a drink of Tom gin; mix this well;
2 lumps of ice,
a bottle of plain soda.
Mix well and serve.

223. Bunch of Violets.

(FOR TWO.)

Put an egg in a mixing-glass,
a spoonful of sugar,
⅙ of benedictine,
⅙ of maraschino,
⅙ of anisette,
⅙ of vino vermouth,
⅙ of crême de vanille,
⅙ of chartreuse,
2 ponies of cream.
Fill your glass with ice; freeze into a jelly, and strain into long glasses, and serve.

224. William's Summer Cooler.

In a very long cut glass the juice of two limes,
a spoonful of powdered sugar,
a good dash of Seltzer; dissolve this well;
1 pony of Santa Cruz rum,
1 glass of California claret; mix this.
Fill your glass with ice; ornament with slices of orange and pineapple, and ice-cream, and top off with strawberries or other berries in season.

225. Whiskey Sling.

A goblet with a little fine ice,
2 dashes of gum,
1 drink of whiskey.
Stir this well, strain and serve.

Medical Drinks.

226.

A handful of fresh tansy is infused in a bottle of gin, this be-ing the best, although other liquors may be used, too; infuse for twenty-four hours at least.   One-third of a drink will be sufficient for a drink, and be a good appetizer.

227.

About a dozen fresh stalks of calamus are infused in a bot-tle of gin for twenty-four hours and served like the former.   It is excellent for cramps.

Introduction to Liquors and Ratafias.

THE manufacture of these alcoholic beverages is done, firstly, by distillation, by which method the finest liquors are obtained; secondly, by extraction, and thirdly, by simply mixing volatile extracts of plants to cognac spirits, etc. They all contain larger or smaller quantities of dissolved sugar, and various aromatic or spicy ingredients.

Distillation is more complicated and troublesome than the two other methods, but it secures products of far higher fineness and value; yet the requirement of the apparatus necessary for manufacturing them renders the application too difficult in a household; furthermore, a profound knowledge of chemistry, great practice and dexterity are required; therefore, this manufacturing is better left to large establishments. The best and most exquisite liquors of this kind are imported from Dantzic, Breslau, Berlin, Stettin, Hamburg, Mannheim, Vienna, Trieste, Amsterdam, Italy, Bordeaux, Paris, and the West Indies. The recipes to manufacture the most famous among them are mostly kept secret; moreover, the foreign ratafias may not easily be imitated because many of the herbs and fruits required for the purpose are not growing in this country.

To prepare good and very palatable liquors for the family use we put down a series of recipes, as verified by our own experience, and that of others. But we declare here candidly and freely, that it is absolutely impossible to obtain by extraction the same liquors as by distillation. The liquors won by infusing fruits or blossoms, or by mixing with fruit-juices are called ratafias; the fine French, very sweet, and, on account of this, more consistent liquors are called crêmes or huiles (oils): *crême de vanille, crême de Barbados, crême de café, de canelle, de chocolat, huile de rose, huile de Venus, de Jupiter, de Cythère, des demoiselles*, etc.

228. Absinthe.

A strong liquor made of vermouth; it is mainly drunk in France; it is said to strengthen the stomach. Swiss absinthe is the most renowned one.

Recipe : To four quarts of cognac spirits take eight ounces of anise, one ounce of star anise, four ounces of great and four ounces of small fennel, one ounce of coriander, one-fourth ounce of angelica root, one ounce of angel sweet root, half an ounce of licorice, half an ounce of calamus, half an ounce of bitter almonds, one ounce of great and one ounce of small leaves of vermouth, one-fourth ounce of peppermint leaves, half an ounce of camilles, one-fourth ounce of juniper; let all these ingredients distill from three to four weeks on a warm place, or in the sunlight; filter and fill into bottles.

229. Almonds' Essence.

One and a half pounds of sweet and four ounces of bitter almonds are poured over with boiling water in a sieve; skin and dry them; grind them very fine by adding from one to one and a half pints of cold water.

Refine three pounds of sugar to what is called *sucre à la plume*, *i.e.*, boil the sugar in water until the sugar, sticking to the wooden spoon can be blown off in bubbles of the size of a pea; add now the ground almonds; let all boil up once, and cool off well covered; press through a hair sieve, fill into small bottles, cork well, and keep them on a cool place.

230. Ananas Cordial.

Cut one-fourth of an unpeeled pineapple into small pieces; boil one quart of water with six ounces of lump-sugar; skin carefully; add the pineapple, and put all in a great stone jar or a demijohn; pour three pints of old Jamaica rum or brandy over it; let it soak a fortnight on a warm place; filter and fill into bottles.

231. Angelica Cordial.

Cut one ounce of fresh or dried angelica into small pieces, put it with one-sixth ounce of cloves, one-sixth ounce of cardamom, one-third ounce of stick cinnamon in a demijohn; pour over it three pints of cognac; let it stand about four weeks in a warm place: sweeten with one pound of lump-sugar refined and cleared in one pint of boiling water.

232. Anisette Cordial.

A fine French cordial; the best one comes from Bordeaux; it is to be warmly recommended after rich dinners, as it helps digestion.

Take six quarts of cognac, four ounces of pulverized star anise, four ounces of ordinary anise, the peel of two lemons, one ounce of stick cinnamon; let this stand four weeks in the sun, or in a warm place; sweeten with two and a half pounds of lump-sugar, refined and cleared in three quarts of boiling water; filter and bottle.

233. Apricot Cordial.

Twenty-five apricots are cut in two; mash their pits, and put all in a stone jar; add half a pound of sugar, six cloves, and half a stick of cinnamon; pour one quart of cognac over it, cover or cork it well; let it stand about three weeks in a warm place, shake it once in a while; filter, and bottle.

234. Arrack.

Arrack is a strong, alcoholic beverage of light yellow color; it is prepared in the East and West Indies from the juice of the areca palm-tree, from the sugary juice of the blossoms of the cocoa palm-tree, which is called toddy, from sugar-molasses or from rice with palm-juice.

The arrack of Goa and Batavia are the best brands and of very delicious odor and taste. The manufacturing is mostly done in very simple, imperfect apparatus, chiefly on Java: the best brand there is called Kiji, the second, Taupo, the last, Sichow.

235. Balm Cordial.

Infuse in one quart of fine cognac a handful of balm-leaves for twenty-four hours in the sunlight or upon the stove; remove the leaves, add one pound of powdered sugar, expose the cordial two days to the sun, until the sugar is all dissolved; filter, and bottle.

236. Basle Kirschwasser.

This well-known, famous liquor is obtained in Switzerland, mainly in the vicinity of Basle and in the Black Forest from the black and very sweet berries of the wood-cherries; gather them when they are very ripe in dry weather; free them from their stalks, and mash them in large tubs with wooden mashers; mash also a part of the pits; then fill the entire substance into casks, each two-thirds full, and cover the bunghole.

The fermentation begins soon, and lasts nearly three weeks; after fermentation is done, bring the whole into a distilling apparatus; continue distilling while slowly heating, until absolutely light, colorless kirschwasser is distilled over to the condenser. This distillate is distilled over again, and filled into bottles.

Many trials have been made to find an equivalent for this excellent cordial, but in vain; never take any but the genuine imported Basle kirschwasser.

237. Bilberry Cordial.

Infuse any quantity of red bilberries in a wide-necked, large bottle with enough cognac to cover them; cork the bottle, place it on a sunny spot, and let it stand until the berries have lost their red color. Filter, add to each quart of liquor one pound of refined sugar-syrup, and bottle.

It is a favorite drink in Sweden and Russia.

238. Benedictine.

The active part of the genuine Benedictine cordial is composed nearly exclusively of plants growing on the steep precipices of Normandy; they are gathered and infused at the time when the sap rises, and the blossoms spring forth. These herbs, growing near the sea, are saturated with bromine, iodine, and chloruret of sodium, and develop and keep their healing power in the alcoholic liquids; only best cognac is used for infusion.

239. Bishop Cordial.

Peel twelve bitter oranges, infuse the rind with one quart of old Jamaica rum or arrack de Batavia in a well-covered tureen for twenty-four hours; strain the fluid, and fill it into small bottles, cork, and seal.

Use two tablespoonfuls of this essence to a bottle of claret, and sweeten to taste.

240. Bitter-Orange Cordial.

Put the rind of six thinly peeled bitter oranges in a stone pot, add the filtered juice of the fruit and two quarts of best brandy;

let it soak for three days, well covered; clear and refine one and a half pounds of sugar, add it to the liquor, filter and bottle; do not use it before six months.

241. Another.

Make with a fine needle little holes in the skin of six bitter oranges, place them in a large bottle; pour in two and a half quarts of brandy; let soak for four weeks, add syrup made of one and a half pounds of sugar and one pint of water; filter and bottle.

242. Cassis Liqueur.

Put one pint of mashed black currants in a big bottle; add half a pound of pulverized sugar and one quart of cognac; cork the bottle well, and let it stand for six weeks in the sun; shake daily; then strain through canton flannel, bottle, and let the bottles lie for a while.

243. Cassis Ratafia.

Put in a stone pot one quart of well-cleaned black currants; mash them, add twenty to thirty raspberries, tied up with some cloves in a little muslin bag; add two and a half quarts of brandy; let it stand for eight weeks; filter; mix it with one pound of sugar refined to syrup, which must be still hot; let it again stand for some days, then filter, and bottle.

244. Chartreuse.

The preparation of this famous cordial and its trade is monopolized by the monks of the monastery Grande Chartreuse, in the French département Isère; the monastery was built by St. Bruno in the year 1086.

The monks keep their secret very carefully; an imitation may be obtained in the following way: Take one pint of the best brandy or kirschwasser, eight drops of vermouth essence, one drop of cinnamon essence, one drop of rose essence, and twelve ounces of sugar that was refined and cleared in one pint of water; strain through flannel, cork, seal, and let it lie at least eight weeks.

245. Cherry Cordial à la Française.

A sufficient quantity, half of sweet and half of sour cherries, is cleaned and mashed; press the juice through a hair-sieve so as to receive two quarts of juice, which is to be poured into a tureen; add one quart of currant-juice, two pounds of powdered sugar, the pits washed and cracked; stir the mixture now and then in order to dissolve the sugar; after this add four quarts of brandy, let soak six days in the well-covered tureen, filter, and bottle.

246. Another.

Put a quantity of very ripe, partly mashed, sour cherries in a tureen; add one-sixth of their weight of ripe, likewise partly mashed raspberries, and a handful of cracked cherry-pits; let it stand a week, then filter the juice; add to each three quarts as much cognac; fill the liquor into a large glass jar; shake often; expose it to the sun for four weeks, filter again, and bottle.

247. English Cherry Brandy.

Twenty pounds of wild cherries are freed of their pits; the pits are pulverized, and with the cherries infused in ten quarts of brandy in a covered stone jar for six weeks; add four pounds of refined sugar, filter, and bottle, but use only after a few months.

248. Another.

Six pounds of wild cherries, six pounds of Armenian cherries, and two pounds of raspberries are mashed and put in a small cask; add three pounds of sugar, twelve cloves, half an ounce of powdered cinnamon, one grated nutmeg, a handful of mint leaves, and seven quarts of fine brandy or gin; bung after ten days, and bottle the brandy after two months.

249. Cherry Ratafia.

For the manufacture of a good and palatable cherry ratafia without a distilling apparatus, we add a couple of recipes:

Fill one and a fourth quarts of brandy, one pound of pulverized sugar, one pound of pulverized sweet and one pound of pulverized sour cherries, half a pint of black currants, one-tenth ounce of cinnamon into a large bottle; expose for three days to the sunlight; filter, bottle, and use after a few weeks.

250. Another.

Eight pounds of sour cherries are freed from their pits, and all are put in a stone pot; add one pound of raspberries, half a pound of currants, one and a half ounces of pulverized almonds, one-fourth ounce of cloves, one-half ounce of powdered cinnamon, one-half ounce of mace; infuse this in four quarts of cognac in a covered pot, for three weeks, on a place that is equally warm; shake daily once, add three pounds of cleared and refined sugar; filter and bottle.

251. Another.

Mash two pounds of sour cherries, put them in a wide-necked bottle, add one quart of cognac, cork well, and let it stand for four weeks.

252. Christophlet.

Grate three-fourths of an ounce of cinnamon, three-fourths ounce of cloves, three-fourths ounce of cardamom, three-fourths ounce of cubebs; put this with one pound of lump-sugar in three pints of claret; cover it well, and let it slowly boil; after cooling add one and a fourth quarts of brandy; strain through canton flannel, bottle, cork, seal, and keep in a dry place.

253. Cinnamon Cordial.

Boil one-fourth pound of roughly pulverized Ceylon cinnamon in one quart of water, half an hour; add one and a half pounds of sugar, and refine it in the cinnamon water; after getting cool mix with one and a half quarts of brandy; cork well, let stand for a few days in a warm place, filter and bottle.

254. Clove Cordial.

Infuse in a big glass jar one-fourth ounce of roughly pulverized cloves, half an ounce of likewise prepared coriander, and a handful of dried cherries in a quart of brandy, five weeks, in the sun or on a warm place; shake daily. Clear and refine five ounces of sugar in half a pint of water; skim very carefully, let it get a little cool, add the infusion and filter through blotting-paper and glass funnel; bottle and let it lie for a few weeks.

255. Coffee Liqueur.

Roast three ounces of the best mocha; grind it; prepare a syrup out of one pound of sugar and half a pound of water; put the coffee in the boiling syrup, and let it boil for a few seconds; mix all with one quart of brandy, cork well, and let it stand for a month; then filter, and the liquor is ready for use.

256. Cognac.

All liquors obtained by distillation of the grape-juice are usually called cognac in France, although only that prepared in the city of Cognac, in the arrondissement of the département Charente, deserves this name; this is the best, while those from Languedoc, Armagnac, Auris, Rochelle, and Bordeaux, are all of inferior quality and less aromatic; but even in the genuine cognac we have to distinguish between many different brands, which depend upon its age, and the results of the wine crop. In France it also has the names " *Trois-six*," corresponding to its percentage of alcohol, and " *Eau de vie*," while the English call it " brandy." Charente and Gironde alone produce yearly more than one million hektoliters (1 hektoliter=105.67 liquid quarts). The fineness of this liquor increases with its age, and when old enough, assumes the taste of an exceedingly fine, spirituous wine. There are many imitations, mostly with spirits of 90° proof, cognac oil and coloring.

257. Curaçao.

This famous liquor is manufactured best in Amsterdam by infusing curaçao peel in very good brandy that has been sweetened with sugar syrup. The curaçao fruit is a species of the bitter orange, that grows mainly in Curaçao, one of the Lesser Antilles, north of Venezuela, and the greatest Dutch colony in the West Indies.

258. Currant Ratafia.

Fill into a large stone pot or jar four quarts of good brandy, two quarts of currant-juice—you obtain this juice by placing the pot with the currants within a larger vessel partly filled with water, which is heated until the currants in the smaller pot burst—add three pounds of sugar, a stick of cinnamon, some cloves; let it stand four weeks; stir daily; filter through flannel, and bottle.

259. Currant Metheglin.

The juice of eight quarts of currants is mixed with twenty quarts of boiling water in which eight pounds of honey are dissolved; add one ounce of cremor tartari; stir well for a quarter of an hour; when the fermentation is over and the liquid is clear, add one quart of brandy; bottle at once, fasten the corks with wire, and place the bottles in the cellar; you may use the beverage after six weeks.

260. English Elder Brandy.

Squeeze the juice of a large quantity of elderberries through a cloth; boil up with sugar and some cloves; let it get cool; add to each twenty quarts of juice two quarts of cognac, and keep it in the cellar.

261. Red English Ratafia.

Four pounds of ripe, red cherries, two pounds of blackberries, three pounds of gooseberries, three pounds of raspberries, three pounds of red currants, are mashed with a wooden masher in a big earthen jug; mash in another pot one-sixteenth ounce of cloves, one-sixteenth ounce of mace, half an ounce of cinnamon, one-third ounce of coriander, one-eighth ounce of fennel, one-sixteenth ounce of Jamaica pepper, the pits of twelve apricots, the pits of twenty sour cherries, and six bitter almonds; mix the two mashes well; add two and a half quarts of sugar syrup, fill all into a large jug, close with a skin, and place it a fortnight near the stove. Then filter the juice through a linen bag, squeeze the remnants well; add one quart of best brandy to each quart of juice; place the mixture again for a fortnight near the stove; filter and bottle.

262. French Ratafia aux Quatre Fruits.

Mash ten pounds of sour cherries, eight pounds of red and two pounds of black currants, and ten pounds of raspberries; let them stand for a few days in the cellar; squeeze the juice, add the same quantity of cognac, and to each quart of the mixture one-fourth pound of refined sugar; mix all well; let the ratafia stand for a week at least; filter and bottle.

263. Another.

Mix one quart of fresh raspberry-juice, one quart of cherry-juice, one quart each of the juice of red and black currants; to each quart of juice add three quarts of cognac, seven ounces of broken lump-sugar, three cloves; expose the mixture in a large glass bottle to the sunlight until it is absolutely clear; filter and bottle.

264. Gin.

A very strong liquor manufactured in Holland (Holland gin), and England (Old Tom gin), which is distilled from juniperus berries, and is used mainly by sailors as a warming beverage, and is good for the stomach, and against scurvy. In Schiedam, Delft and Rotterdam, gin is manufactured in large quantities; in Schiedam there are more than 300 distilleries.

265. Ginger Cordial.

In a large, wide-necked bottle place one and a half ounces of pulverized ginger; infuse this in a quart of cognac, well corked, for from two to three days; stir now and then; strain through a flannel, and add a syrup of one pound of sugar cleared and refined in one gill of water; filter again; cork well.

The English often add to the pulverized ginger one pound of mashed black or white currants that secures a very delicious taste.

266. Gingerette.

One pound of very ripe black currants are cleaned from their stalks, and infused with one quart of gin, and the rind of a thinly peeled lemon three days in a well-corked bottle; strain the liquor into another bottle; add half an ounce of pulverized ginger, and one pound of granulated sugar; place the bottle in a sunny spot; shake it daily; strain the liquor once more into smaller bottles, cork well, and let them lie for a while before using.

267. Grenoble Ratafia.

Mash a quantity of very ripe sour cherries with a wooden masher, pits included; let the mash soak forty-eight hours in a clean wooden tub, then squeeze the juice. Refine the sugar, two pounds to every six or seven quarts, add the sugar syrup to the juice, one-third ounce of cloves, two-thirds of an ounce of broken cinnamon, two handfuls of fresh sour cherry leaves, and six quarts of cognac; pour everything into a small cask, which, while daily shaken, has to lie four to six weeks; bottle the ratafia after filtering; use after a while.

268. Hip Liqueur.

Infuse one and a half pounds of fresh, well-cleaned hips, cut into pieces, in one quart of kirschwasser a fortnight in a warm place; refine and clear six ounces of sugar in half a pint of boiling water; let this get cool, and mix it with the liquor; strain it through blotting-paper, and bottle it.

269. English Hop Ratafia.

A wide-necked bottle is filled with ripe, dried cones of the hop; shake them together without pressing, infuse it with sherry for four weeks; strain and mix it with a thin sugar syrup of six ounces of sugar with half a pint of water; strain again, bottle and seal; use either unmixed or with water as a tonic for the stomach.

270. Irish Usquebaugh.

(SEE WHISKEY.)

This famous cordial, which the French call Scubac, is prepared in various ways.

One and one-fifth ounces of nutmeg, as much of cloves and of cinnamon, two and one-third ounces of anise, as much of kümmel and coriander are mashed; put this with four ounces of licorice root, twenty-three quarts of rectified alcohol, and four and a half quarts of water in the distilling apparatus; color the condensated liquor with saffron, and sweeten with sugar syrup.

271. Another.

Infuse one ounce of grated nutmeg, as much of cinnamon, angelica, rhubarb and cassia; one-third ounce of saffron, as much of cardamom, cloves and mace; one-third ounce of coriander, as much of anise and kümmel, and three and one-third ounces of licorice root in twenty-three quarts of brandy a fortnight; filter the liquor; sweeten with sugar syrup, filter again and bottle; use after a few months.

272. Another.

In smaller quantities this liquor is prepared by Irish house-wives as follows :

Infuse one pound of seedless raisins, half an ounce of grated nutmeg, one-fourth of an ounce of pulverized cloves, as much of cardamom, the peel of a sour orange rubbed off on sugar, half a pound of brown rock-candy, and a little saffron tincture in two quarts of brandy a fortnight; stir daily; filter and bottle.

273. Iva Liqueur.

This is very good, green bitters, which is obtained in Switzerland out of the *Achillea Moschata*, a shrub that grows on the highest Alps; it is of great aromatic odor and taste, and a great article for export.

274. Juniper Cordial.

Mash slightly half a pint of fresh juniper berries; infuse it with four quarts of cognac a fortnight in a large glass bottle; expose it to the sunlight; filter; mix with a syrup of one and a half pounds of sugar in three-fourths of a quart of water; cork well; let the mixture stand for a few days; filter and bottle.

275. Kajowsky.

(SLOE RATAFIA.)

After you have plucked, at the end of September a sufficient quantity of very ripe sloes, spread them on a sheet of paper, lay them one day in the sun, then take the pits out, wash them and dry them in the sun. For each half a pint of pits take one quart of cognac; break the pits, and put shells and pits in the cognac; let it stand for six weeks; shake now and then. Filter after this time, and fill into a large, flat tureen, then boil for each quart of liquor three pounds of loaf-sugar over a fast fire to a brownish syrup; add this carefully, while stirring, to the liquor; continue stirring until both liquids are well mixed, bottle, cork and seal.

(The longer you let it lie, the better your liquor will become.)

276. Kümmel.

Fill three quarts of cognac or kirschwasser, six ounces of broken caraway, and two-fifths of an ounce of star anise into a glass bottle, close it with a bladder, and place it in a pot partly filled with cold water; now heat this, and let boil for half an hour; take the pot from the fire, and let the bottle get cool in the water, then sweeten the liquor with two pounds of refined sugar; filter, bottle and cork well.

277. Another.

With the aid of oils the method of manufacturing is as follows:

> dissolve 30 drops of caraway extract,
>
> 2 drops of fennel oil,
>
> 1 drop of cinnamon oil in one ounce of spirits;

mix this to four quarts of cognac and three pounds of refined sugar; filter and bottle.

278. Lemon Ratafia.

Infuse the thinly peeled rind of four or five lemons with two quarts of cognac or kirschwasser in a corked bottle, for twelve days, in a moderately warm place; boil one and a half pounds of lump-sugar in two quarts of water until the sugar drops from the wooden spoon in large flakes; add the spirit, let it simmer over a slow fire for a few minutes, strain through flannel, and bottle after cooling.

279. English Lemon Ratafia.

Four quarts of cognac are filled into a stone jar with one and a half pounds of pulverized sugar, the juice and the rind of sixteen lemons, and two quarts of boiling milk; stir thoroughly; cover the pot and let it stand for ten days; stir the fluid daily; then strain it through flannel, and bottle.

280. Magenbitters.

Three ounces of bitter-orange peel, three-fourths of an ounce of star anise, one-fourth of an ounce of ordinary anise, half an ounce of gentian, half an ounce of alant root, one-fourth ounce of *Erythræa Centaurium*, and one-fourth ounce of cremor tartari; infuse these ingredients in four quarts of cognac two to three weeks; filter, sweeten with two pounds of refined sugar and bottle.

281. Another.

Three ounces of orange-peel, one-fourth ounce of vermouth, one-fourth ounce of *Erythræa Centaurium*, one-eighth ounce of angelica root, one-fourth ounce of violet roots, one-fourth ounce of *Carduus Benedictus*, one-eighth ounce of stick cinnamon, one-eighth ounce of grated nutmeg; infuse these ingredients in two quarts of cognac from two to three weeks; sweeten with one pound of refined sugar, and bottle.

282. Maraschino.

One of the finest liquors which is prepared in Italy and Dalmatia from the berry of the mahaleb cherry, equally excellent for its odor and taste; this fruit is black, berry-like, flat above and oval below; it tastes bitter, but contains a pit of great fragrance. When these fruits are perfectly ripe, they are gathered, and mashed together with the pits; best white honey of their own weight is added; the fluid undergoes first a fermentation, and is then subject to distillation. This first distillate has to lie for a year; then it is distilled twice more, and is now a very delicious liquor, which, however, is but the basis of the real maraschino di Zara. Take, now, sugar one-third of the liquor's weight, dissolve it in one-third of its weight of water; refine this sugar syrup by the white of one egg or more; boil it to the consistency of a thick syrup, filter through a flannel bag, and mix this with the liquor; bottle, let the bottles lie for a year, and they are filled then into the well-known straw-covered bottles that are exported from Trieste, Austria.

There is a number of recipes to imitate this cordial, but we must abstain from publishing them, as being too difficult to prepare.

283. Mint Liqueur.

Infuse two handfuls of fresh mint leaves in two quarts of the best brandy, three or four weeks, in a well-corked bottle, in the sun or in a warm place; add a cold syrup of three-fourths to one pound of sugar; filter and bottle.

284. Nalifka.

A kind of a light fruit liquor; it is made mostly of berries and cherries, but also of plums and apples, and is very highly estimated in Russia, and prepared there in almost all houses, especially in the country. The best nalifkas are won of the *Rubus Chamæmorus*, which grows only in Russia, Norway, Sweden, East Prussia, and the northern part of England, of the black and red currants, of the berries of the mountain ash, and of cherries. All these fruits must be very ripe; those of the mountain must not be gathered before the first frost.

Fill a big glass jar two-thirds full with berries, and pour over it cognac to fill the jar; close the jar with a piece of muslin; expose it from two to three months to the direct action of the sunlight, and shake every second or third day. Then filter the nalifka through a funnel covered with linen and absorbent cotton, until it flows off perfectly clear; fill into ordinary wine bottles. Add to each three or four bottles of nalifka one bottle of water, and to each bottle of the thinned liquor four ounces of sugar that has been refined in boiling water to a consistent syrup. Add to this syrup the whole quantity of nalifka, heat the fluid, while constantly stirring, nearly to the boiling-point; take it from the fire, and pour it into an earthen or china pot. After cooling, bottle, cork and seal; you may either use it right away, or keep it.

285. Nonpareil Liqueur.

Peel a perfectly ripe pineapple, cut it into slices and mash them; add twenty of the best white plums, cut in two, and without the pits—and one dozen of very aromatic pears. To each four pounds of fruit take six pounds of loaf-sugar, and one and a half quarts of water; boil all this for three-quarters of an hour in an enameled pot; pour it into a tureen, add three quarts of fine cognac, cover it air-tight, let it stand for six weeks, filter through a jelly-bag, and bottle.

286. Noyeau.

A very fine cordial; the genuine article comes from Martinique only, and is very rare and expensive; only small quantities of it must be taken, as it is not harmless at all in spite of its unique taste. It is prepared from the pits of a fruit in the West Indies, and these pits contain a strong dose of hydrocyanic acid.

The French prepare a number of very good imitations of the genuine noyeau. For those that are in possession of a distilling apparatus we add a very good French recipe:

Half a pound of cut apricot-pits are infused in six quarts of rectified alcohol, and one quart of water, for a week; distil the alcohol, mix it with one pint of orange-flower water, and three pounds of sugar that is cleared and refined in three quarts of water, filter and fill into bottles; use it after a few months.

287. English Orange Brandy.

Two pounds of lump-sugar, ten whole oranges, and one stick of cinnamon are put in five quarts of the best brandy; let it stand in a well-covered stone jar from five to six weeks, and stir it daily with a wooden spoon; filter and fill into bottles.

288. Orange-Flower Ratafia.

Three and a half ounces of fresh orange-flowers are infused in two quarts of the best brandy in a sunny place four days; filter; add a syrup of one and a half pounds of sugar in one quart of water; filter again and bottle.

289. Orange Liquor.

Peel six oranges thinly with a sharp knife, put the peel in two quarts of cognac; press the juice of the oranges on two and a half pounds of lump-sugar, which is to be added to the liquor right away after melting; let it stand five to six weeks, daily stirring with a wooden spoon; filter and fill into bottles.

290. Parfait Amour.

A very fine cordial which may be made in different ways.

If you have a distilling apparatus, distil three quarts of alcohol with the rind of four thinly peeled lemons, one-fifteenth ounce of lemon oil, one-thirtieth ounce of bergamot oil; stop when the distillate shows 60° to 70° Tralles; distil anew with one quart of milk, dye the entire distillate with cochineal tinctures lightly red, and add two quarts of sugar syrup.

BY INFUSION.

Ten drops of clove essence, five drops of nutmeg essence, and a few drops of lemon essence are mixed with two quarts of alcohol of 83°; color with cochineal tincture slightly red, and add a syrup out of four pounds of sugar in one quart of water. Let the mixture stand four weeks; stir or shake daily, then filter and bottle.

291. Another.

Mash three fine peeled celery roots with the green sprigs on them; add four and a half quarts of brandy; distil this mixture with a spoonful of salt in a retort. The obtained product is mixed with three-fourths of a pound of roasted and pulverized cocoa beans, one-fourth of an ounce of cut vanilla, and three pounds of refined sugar; let it stand for a week; color with a cochineal tincture slightly red, and filter.

292. Persico.

This fine cordial must be taken only in small doses, as it contains hydrocyanic acid. Peel half a pound of peach-pits, and half a pound of apricot-pits, mash them, and infuse the mash with one-eighth of an ounce of fine cinnamon in four quarts of cognac; infuse in a large bottle a week in the sun; filter; purify two pounds of loaf-sugar in one pint of water, strain, and let it get cool; mix this syrup with the liquor, and fill into bottles.

293. Another.

Put one and a fourth pounds of fresh peach-kernels in luke-warm water, skin and mash them; infuse the mash with one-eighth of an ounce of broken cinnamon and four quarts of best brandy in a jug for four weeks; cover the jug with a skin; after this make a syrup of two pounds of sugar and one pint of water, and filter the whole mixture through a jelly-bag; bottle.

294. Quince Liquor.

A number of very ripe, fine quinces are peeled, grated, and left over night in the cellar; the following day squeeze the juice; take to each four and a half quarts of quince-juice two quarts of cognac, one pound of sugar, one ounce of stick cinnamon, two-fifths of an ounce of cloves, and two ounces of pulverized bitter almonds; let all this stand in a well-corked bottle a fortnight; shake daily and filter.

295. Another.

Grate the quinces, let them stand twenty-four hours; squeeze the juice; refine one pound of sugar in three pints of water, add the syrup, and let all boil for a quarter of an hour; let it get cool; add the same quantity of brandy or kirschwasser, pour all into a large glass bottle, add one ounce of bitter almonds, and one and one-third ounces of coriander; let soak a fortnight; shake daily, filter and bottle.

296. English Quince Liquor.

After you have cleaned a few ripe quinces with a towel, cut them in two, cut out the seeds, and grate the fruit on a grater, place the mash lightly strewed with sugar in a large dish twenty-four hours in a cool place; squeeze the juice, filter until it is perfectly clear; add to each pint of juice half a pound of sugar, and one pint of brandy or whiskey; let the liquor stand a fortnight; shake daily and bottle.

297. French Quince Ratafia.

Very ripe, well-cleaned quinces are grated on a grater; let the mash stand three days in a well-covered earthen dish in the cellar, and squeeze the juice out. Add to the filtered juice an equal quantity of brandy, seven ounces of sugar to each quart of the mixture, a stick of cinnamon, and a few cloves; let soak two months, filter, fill into bottles and let them lie as long as possible, as the aroma is thus highly improved.

298. Raspberry Ratafia.

In a large glass bottle infuse one quart of fresh and very ripe raspberries with two quarts of cognac; close the bottle well, and let it stand in the sun four weeks; then refine two pounds of sugar in one quart of boiling water to a thin syrup; add the syrup to the liquor; strain through flannel, and bottle.

299. French Raspberry Ratafia.

Put in a tureen four quarts of cognac, two quarts of raspberry-juice, two pounds of loaf-sugar, a few sticks of cinnamon, and four or five cloves; stir it well; cover and let it stand four weeks in a warm place; strain and bottle.

300. Rose Ratafia.

One-fourth of a pound of fresh aromatic roses (leaves only) are shaken in a vessel with one pint of lukewarm water; cover well, and place aside for two days, then filter the water, and press the roses gently; mix the rose-water with the same quantity of kirschwasser; add to each quart of the mixture half a pound of refined sugar, a few coriander-kernels, and a little fine cinnamon; let the whole soak in the sun a fortnight, add some cochineal tincture for coloring, filter and bottle.

301. Rosoglio.

It is the name of several fine cordials, imported from Italy; they are prepared of orange-flowers, or other flowers and fruits, spices, etc., and exported in straw bottles from Turin, Naples, Venice, Bologna, Udine and Trieste.

An imitation of such a rosoglio is made as follows: clear and refine four pounds of sugar in one and a fourth quarts of water; mix two quarts of best alcohol of 83°, eight drops of rose essence, two drops of cinnamon essence, two drops of lemon essence, two drops of Portugal essence, a few drops of cochineal tincture to color, with the sugar syrup; let it stand four weeks in a large bottle; filter and fill into smaller bottles.

302. Rum.

Genuine rum is a very fine liquor; it is manufactured in the West Indies out of the juice of the sugar cane, and the relics of the sugar production, as molasses and syrup: it is used all over the world for punches, grogs, teas, etc. The best rum is that of Jamaica, but the brands of St. Croix, British Guiana, Barbadoes, Antigua, and others, although they are inferior to the Jamaica rum, are very palatable. The quality of rum is best known from its aroma, its pleasing taste, and its alcohol which must amount to 58° to 66° Tralles; the best and simplest proof is, when rum is diluted in hot water or tea; then the fineness of the aroma is developed, or by rubbing a few drops between the hands.

303. Rum Liquor.

Peel the rind of two or three bitter oranges very thin; let soak for two days in one pint of cold water, filter, and refine two pounds of sugar in it; add one pint of cleared juice of the oranges, and one and a half quarts of old Jamaica rum; filter the liquor, bottle, and keep it for future use.

304. Saffron Liquor.

In a big, well-corked jug half an ounce of best saffron, one-fourth of a pound of pulverized sugar, half an ounce of broken cinnamon, half an ounce of cloves, half an ounce of Jamaica pepper, half an ounce of nutmeg (cloves, pepper, and nutmeg roughly pulverized), one ounce of sweet almonds, one-fourth of an ounce of bitter ones (both skinned and mashed with a little alcohol), one ounce of caraway, are infused in three-fourths of a quart of water and as much of the best brandy, for a fortnight; strain until perfectly clear, bottle, cork and seal; let them lie in the cellar—the longer, the better.

305. Stomach Essence.

One and a half pounds of *cortex Chinæ*, six ounces of curaçao peel, one ounce of *flores Cassiæ* are infused in four quarts of cognac from two to three weeks; filter the fluid, sweeten with two pounds of refined sugar, and bottle.   (The sweetening may be omitted.)

306. Strawberry Liquor.

Fill into a large glass jar one pound of fresh strawberries, half a pound of white rock-candy (pulverized), and one and a half quarts of cognac; cork and seal well; let it stand in the sun for five weeks; shake daily, then strain the liquor through blotting-paper, and bottle.

307. Sweet Calamus Liquor.

Infuse four ounces of dried, thinly cut sweet calamus, and a little over an ounce of cut angelica in two and one-half quarts of cognac, in a well-corked, large bottle, for four weeks, in a rather warm place; clear and refine two pounds of lump-sugar in one and a half quarts of water; mix it with the liquor, filter, and bottle.

308. Vanilla Liquor.

Infuse two and a half sticks of vanilla in four quarts of brandy a fortnight; refine two pounds of sugar in four quarts of water to syrup, add the liquor; mix well over a slow fire, filter, and bottle.

309. Another.

Cut four sticks of vanilla into very small pieces, put them in a bottle with three quarts of best brandy; let infuse a fortnight, shake daily, add two pounds of refined sugar, let the liquor stand a few days, color slightly red with cochineal-tincture, and bottle.

310. Vespetro.

An Italian cordial. One-fourth of an ounce of angelica seeds, three-fourths of an ounce of coriander, one-fourth of an ounce of fennel, one-fourth of an ounce of anise, the juice and the thin peel of two lemons, and one pound of sugar are infused in two quarts of brandy five or six days, in a warm place; filter and bottle.

311. Walnut Liquor.

One pound of green walnuts gathered at the end of June or beginning of July, is cut in small pieces, and in a jug or a glass jar infused in two and a half quarts of fine brandy with one-eighth ounce of pulverized cinnamon, and as much of cloves, from six to eight weeks; cork well, and shake daily. After this time filter the infusion, add syrup of one pound of sugar and one quart of water: filter again and bottle.

312. Another.

Infuse one pound of cut green walnuts in two quarts of fine cognac, in the sun, a fortnight; filter into another bottle, add half an ounce of cinnamon, and one-fourth of an ounce of roughly pulverized cloves; let it stand another week in the sun; add a syrup of three-fourths of a pound of sugar and one pint of water; mix well, filter, and bottle; after half a year it is ready for use.

313. Whiskey Cordial.

A liquor which is made in English families, when the white currants are getting perfectly ripe.

Infuse the rind of a thinly peeled lemon, half a pint of white currants (a little mashed), and a small piece of ginger in a quart of whiskey, twenty-four hours, in a warm place; filter, sweeten with half a pound of refined sugar, filter again, and bottle.

314. Wild-Cherry Essence.

A quantity of very ripe, wild cherries are pressed through an earthen sieve with a wooden spoon, so that only the pits remain; pulverize them with a few bitter almonds; mix them with the cherry mash, and let the mixture stand two days in a cool place. After this time squeeze the juice thoroughly, let it stand for another day, strain carefully through flannel, boil it for a few seconds with lump-sugar—one pound to one quart of juice—filter again, and after cooling, bottle well and seal, and keep the bottles in a cool place.

A few spoonfuls of this extract flavor a bottle of claret or a bowl exceedingly well.

315. Whiskey.

It derives its name from the obsolete Irish word "Usquebah" or "Usquebaugh" (water of life). Another whiskey in Scotland is called "Mountain Dew." It is made from barley, but often other grains are substituted for it.

316. Peach and Apple Brandies.

They are domestic products from the juice of the corresponding fruits, and chiefly made in Maryland and New Jersey. As they are sold at high prices much adulteration is going on in them.

Punches.

317. Admiral.

Boil one bottle of claret with one-half pound of sugar, a stick of cinnamon, and a piece of vanilla for a quarter of an hour; add the yolks of six eggs that have first been beaten in a tumbler of cold wine; beat the drink into foam over the fire, and serve it in cups.

318. Ale Flip.

This is a kind of warm beer which is very fashionable in England during the winter, and it is taken by sportsmen early in the morning before starting for the hunt. The recipe follows: one and a half quarts of ale, a spoonful of sugar, a piece of mace, half a dozen of cloves, and a small piece of butter, and let it boil; then beat the white of one egg with the yolks of two or three eggs in a spoonful of cold ale, add it to the boiling ale, and pour the whole swiftly from one vessel into another for a few minutes, then serve.

319. Ale Punch.

Take one quart of Burton ale, one glass of Niersteiner, a wineglassful of brandy, a wineglassful of capillaire syrup, the juice of a lemon, a piece of lemon-peel; grate a little nutmeg, add a piece of toast; mix everything well; let it stand cold for from two to three hours; strain, and serve.

320. Alliance de Neufchâtel.

Take the yolks of eight eggs, stir with one pound of pulverized sugar and the juice of two oranges; heat two bottles of claret with a stick of vanilla to the boiling-point; add the wine under continuous beating to the eggs and sugar, and pour the foamy drink into champagne glasses.

321. Alymeth.

Boil one bottle of Burgundy with one pound of lump-sugar, half a stick of cinnamon, a little bit of mace and coriander, and two bay-leaves; light with a burning paper, and let it burn until it goes out by itself; then fill it into glasses, and drink it warm.

322. American Punch.

Rub the peel of six lemons on one pound of sugar; squeeze the juice of the lemons and that of six oranges on it; remove the seeds carefully; add four pounds of loaf-sugar, and five cloves and two leaves of mace tied up in a piece of linen, likewise two quarts of water; refine the sugar to syrup; skim well, fill into bottles, and keep for the punch. Now mix three-fourths of a quart of green tea, one pint of cognac, one quart of old Jamaica rum, one bottle of champagne, and a cup of chartreuse well sweetened to taste with the syrup, pour it into a punch-bowl, add a big lump of ice, three oranges cut in slices, and three lemons without the seeds; let the beverage stand for two hours, stir repeatedly, and serve.

323. Ananas Punch.

Dissolve two and one-half pounds of lump-sugar in three quarts of boiling water, add three bottles of Rhine wine, one bottle of old Jamaica rum, and two bottles of champagne; let it stand on a warm stove for an hour, and add finally the juice of a mashed ananas (pineapple). Keep the vessel well covered or the aroma will escape.

324. Ananas Punch à l'Amérique.

(FOR TEN PERSONS.)

Peel and cut four pineapples of medium size, put the slices with one pound of pulverized sugar in a bowl, and let it stand well covered on a cool place, until the sugar has gone entirely into the slices; add one pint of old Jamaica rum, one pint of best brandy, one gill of curaçao, and the juice of four lemons; place a big piece of ice in the middle of the bowl; add four bottles of champagne, and serve in champagne glasses.

325. Arrack Foam.

Mix one quart of sour cream with half a pint of arrack, and four ounces of lump-sugar; beat it to foam, and serve it in glasses.

326. Arrack Punch.

Rub the peel of three or four lemons on twelve ounces of loaf-sugar, break the sugar, and dissolve it in one quart of strong, boiling tea; add the juice of six or eight lemons, and a pint of good arrack.

327. Another.

Cut six unpeeled lemons into thin slices; remove their seeds; infuse them in one pint of arrack six hours; take them out carefully with a fork without squeezing them, then dissolve one pound of lump-sugar in three pints of boiling water, add the arrack, let the beverage get cool, and serve in small glasses.

328. Beer Punch.

Boil one quart of beer with one-fourth of a pound of lump-sugar and a stick of cinnamon; beat four eggs into foam, and mix it with a wineglassful of old Jamaica rum; take the beer from the fire and add to it the mixture while continually stirring it; serve in punch glasses.

329. Beer Chaudeau.

Stir two whole eggs in a glass of wine; pour this into a pint of beer; add a teaspoonful of sugar, a stick of cinnamon, and a piece of lemon-peel; beat the whole over a fire to foam, fill it into cups, and serve.

330. Beer Grog.

Beat four eggs, pour them into one quart of beer, add one-fourth of a pound of sugar, a little cinnamon and lemon-peel; put all over a fast fire, and beat continually, until it begins to rise, without letting it boil; take it from the fire, continue beating for a few minutes, and fill into glasses.

331. English Brandy Punch.

Put the rind of two lemons in a pot with a stick of cinnamon, three-fourths of a pound of lump-sugar, some mace, and three cloves to one-half of a pint of water; let it boil slowly for ten minutes, strain it, add one bottle of brandy and the juice of the two lemons, pour into a tureen, light it, and let it burn for five minutes before filling the punch into glasses.

332. Bristol Punch.

To each quart of boiling water take the juice of one and a half lemons, the rind of half a lemon, three gills of rum, and sugar to taste. Put sugar, juice and peel in a bowl, pour over it enough water to dissolve the sugar, and to extract the aroma; after half an hour remove the peel, and add water and rum.

333. Burning Punch.

A bottle of claret, one and a half bottles of Rhine wine, one pound of sugar, and a little over one pint of rum are heated nearly to the boiling-point; take it from the fire before it boils; light with burning paper, and when the flame goes out add some hot water or tea, if you desire.

334. English Burned Punch.

Rub the rind of three lemons lightly on one pound of sugar, put the sugar in an earthen pot, and pour over it one quart of rum and one quart of claret; stir all well over a fire, until it begins to boil and the sugar is dissolved; add one quart of boiling water, and the juice of three lemons. This punch may be taken warm or cold.

335. Campichello Punch.

Heat slowly the yolks of twelve eggs with two pounds of lump-sugar on which you have rubbed off the rind of two oranges, their juice and that of three lemons, and three bottles of claret; beat it to foam until it begins to boil; then add carefully a bottle of old Jamaica rum, and serve at once.

336. Champagne Punch.

Boil one and one-half pounds of lump-sugar in three pints of water, add the juice of five lemons, half a bottle of arrack, and one bottle of champagne; heat it sufficiently, and serve

337. Champagne Crême.

Beat half a pound of pulverized sugar with the yolks of eight eggs and five whole eggs to the form of frozen snow; add, while continually beating, the rind of an orange, rubbed off on sugar, and gradually a quart-bottle of champagne; heat over a slow fire, while continually beating, and serve warm.

338. The Chat.

Boil a large pot of mixed tea; a little sugar in the bottom of a hot cup, two-thirds full of tea; fill the rest with Burgundy, and serve. If desired, add a little vanilla to the tea.

339. English Claret Punch.

Boil, in half a pint of water, half a pound of lump-sugar with one-fifth of an ounce of cinnamon, one-tenth of an ounce of pulverized ginger, and as many pulverized cloves, and the thinly peeled rind of an orange, to syrup; skim this with a wooden spoon, and add two bottles of claret; take the vessel from the fire before the wine begins to boil.

340. Cold Claret Punch.

One bottle of claret, half a pint of sherry, half a wineglassful of maraschino, the rind of a lemon, one-quarter of a pound of pulverized sugar, and a sprig of borage; let this all stand for an hour, strain the punch through a sieve, add a piece of ice and a bottle of Seltzer.

Instead of the rind of the lemon and the borage, you may add fresh raspberries and cut peaches, when these fruits are in season.

341. Claret Punch.

Pour two bottles of claret into an enameled pot, squeeze the juice of three lemons, add one pound of sugar; heat the wine to the boiling-point without letting it boil, take it from the fire, and add half a bottle of best arrack.

342. Confession of Love.

Infuse half an ounce of fine black tea in half a pint of boiling water for five minutes; decant and pour it into a tureen; rub the rind of a lemon on three pounds of lump-sugar, refine in one pint of boiling water; skim well; add a piece of vanilla, cut into small pieces, and half an ounce of dried orange-flowers; take the sugar from the fire, and leave vanilla and orange-flowers one hour in it; then strain through a sieve into a tureen. Now add a wineglassful of maraschino, the juice of five oranges, two bottles of Rhine wine, two bottles of Médoc, one bottle of Madeira, and one bottle of arrack; let the mixture get very hot, without boiling, and serve it hot; it is still better when very cold.

343. Crambambuli.

Pour one bottle of arrack into a pot, light the fluid with burning paper, and melt one pound of lump-sugar over this flame, so as to make the melting sugar drop into the fluid.

344. Cream Punch à l'Amérique.

Beat the yolks of six eggs with one pound of powdered sugar; add half a bottle of fine rum or arrack; beat one and a half quarts of milk and the whites of the six eggs to a consistent foam; mix both ingredients together, and beat again.

(This drink is very palatable, especially for ladies.)

345. Currant Shrub.

It is a kind of punch essence which, in combination with cold or hot water, furnishes a very delicious drink.

Two quarts of currants are put in a pot which is placed in a larger one partly filled with water; let it slowly boil until the berries burst and the juice flows out; skim well and filter; to each pint of juice take three-fourths pound of sugar; dissolve it well, and add one quart of old Jamaica rum; filter the mixture again, bottle, and seal.

346. Egg Grog.

Boil one quart of water with half a pound of sugar; beat the yolks of five eggs in one pint of St. Croix rum, and add this, while continually stirring, to the boiling water.

347. Egg Punch.

Six eggs, and the yolks of ten eggs are well stirred in a new enameled pot, with one and one-fourth pounds of powdered sugar; add, while continually stirring, one bottle of Rhine wine and one quart of cold water; put over a coal-fire, and beat until it boils; add the juice of two oranges and of two lemons, and half a bottle of arrack; beat again until boiling, strain through a sieve, and serve.

348. Egg Liquor.

Put in a tureen the yolks of twelve fresh eggs, one pound of pulverized sugar, a small teaspoonful of powdered cinnamon, and a little grated nutmeg; place the tureen on ice; beat the yolks to foam, and add, while beating, one pint of kirschwasser and three pints of sweet cream; beat the mixture for another quarter of an hour, strain through a sieve, and serve in glasses.

349. Egg Milk Punch.

Infuse a stick of vanilla in one quart of boiling milk; strain the milk, add six ounces of sugar and one quart of sweet cream: let this boil up once more; stir into it the yolks of five or six eggs; let the fluid get cool, and add one pint of Santa Cruz rum.

350. Egg-Nogg Punch.

Beat well the yolks of four eggs in a tureen with six ounces of powdered sugar; add gradually one pint of fine brandy, one-fifth of a pint of Santa Cruz rum, one pony of maraschino, and two quarts of milk; beat the whites of the eggs till they assume a light, snowy appearance, and sweeten with a little vanilla or lemon sugar; let the whites float on top of the mixture; put it on ice, and serve cold.

351. Egg Punch.

Take one bottle of Rhine wine, the juice of two lemons and their peel rubbed on six ounces of lump-sugar, ten eggs, and nine ounces of pulverized sugar; stir all well; place the pot in a vessel partly filled with boiling water, beat the mixture to a thick foam, and add finally half a pint of warmed arrack.

352. Cold Egg Punch.

Pour three-fourths of a quart of boiling water on one ounce of fine black tea; let it stand for about six minutes; strain the tea, sweeten with four ounces of sugar, add the well-beaten yolks of five eggs, and stir thoroughly; fill it into a freezing-can, and turn it in the ice-cream freezer for ten minutes; add the juice of two lemons and two oranges, and turn again for a quarter of an hour; three-quarters of an hour before serving the punch begin anew to turn and stir the whole mixture, so as to make it flowing and foamy. Finally beat the whites of the five eggs to foam; mix it with one-fourth pound of sugar, add it to the punch, and half a pint of Santa Cruz rum, and serve in glasses.

353. Cold Egg Wine.

The yolks of seven fresh eggs are stirred with two ounces of powdered sugar and a teaspoonful of lemon-juice; add this to two quarts of cold Rhine wine while briskly and continually stirring.

354. Egg Wine.

One pint of white wine, the yolks of two fresh eggs, two ounces of pulverized sugar, are well mixed, and beaten over fire until the wine rises.

355. Another.

Boil one pint of Rhine wine, half a pint of water, and two ounces of sugar; meanwhile stir the yolks of two eggs in two tablespoonfuls of cold water; add the boiling wine while continually beating or stirring, and serve in glasses.

356. English Punch.

Rub the rind of two large lemons on half a pound of sugar; put it in a tureen, squeeze the juice of the fruit on it, pour one quart of boiling water over it; stir all well; add three gills of rum, half a pint of best brandy; grate a little nutmeg, heat it over a coal fire, but do not let it boil, and fill into glasses.

357. Another.

Rub the rind of two lemons, and of one bitter orange on seven ounces of sugar; put it in a tureen, squeeze the juice of the fruit over it, add one and a half pints of boiling water, stir until the sugar is dissolved, add one pint of rum, half a pint of brandy, and two tablespoonfuls of noyeau, and serve in glasses.

358. Another.

One ounce of tea is steeped in two quarts of boiling water; strain the tea over three-fourths pound of lump-sugar, on which the rind of four or five bitter oranges has been rubbed off; add a bottle of Santa Cruz rum, and serve.

359. Fletsch.

Rub the rind of three lemons on twelve ounces of lump-sugar, add two quarts of boiling water, and three quarts of hot claret, and serve as soon as the sugar is dissolved.

360. Flip.

One and a half quarts of beer are heated to boiling, with a stick of cinnamon, a small piece of ginger, two or three cloves, and some lemon-peel; meanwhile mix the yolks of four eggs with a large wineglassful of rum or arrack, two or three tablespoonfuls of pulverized sugar, and a small spoonful of corn-starch; add this, while continually stirring, to the beer; pour it a few times from one vessel into another, strain through a sieve, and serve in cups.

361. Fruit Punch.

Boil three quarts of water with twelve ounces of sugar, and the juice of two or three lemons: mix this in a tureen with one quart of Santa Cruz rum or arrack, and one quart of raspberry or cherry syrup.

362. George IV. Punch.

On seven ounces of sugar rub the peel of two lemons, and of two bitter oranges; put in a tureen with the juice of the fruits; let it stand for half an hour; add one cup of boiling water, and stir until the sugar is dissolved. Add one pint of green tea, half a pint of pineapple syrup, a wineglassful of maraschino, four tablespoonfuls of the best arrack, one pint of brandy, and a bottle of champagne; mix all, put on ice, and serve.

363. German Tea Punch.

Heat one quart of white beer with a little stick of cinnamon, add a spoonful of corn-starch dissolved in wine; stir rapidly; add half a bottle of Rhine wine, six ounces of sugar, and the juice of half a lemon; heat all once more to the boiling-point; beat the yolks of four eggs with it; sweeten with one pound of sugar on which you have previously rubbed off the rind of half a lemon; add a pony of maraschino, and serve in cups.

364. Another.

Heat two quarts of white beer, beat in it the yolks of six eggs; add three-fourths pound of sugar, on which you have rubbed the rind of half a lemon, and half a bottle of white wine; heat the mixture again, while continually beating, but do not let it boil; add half a wineglassful of maraschino, and the juice of a lemon; serve very foamy in cups.

365. Gin Punch.

Peel the rind of a large lemon very thin, put it with a tablespoonful of the juice of a lemon in a tureen, add two tablespoonfuls of powdered sugar, and one pint of cold water, and let it stand for half an hour; afterward add half a pint of the best Holland gin, a wineglassful of maraschino, three or four lumps of ice, two bottles of plain soda, and serve at once.

366. Giroflée.

Boil two bottles of Médoc with one pound of lump-sugar, one stick of cinnamon, and some cloves for a few minutes

367. Glasgow Punch.

Put half a pound of pulverized sugar, and the rind of half a thinly peeled lemon with the juice of two large lemons in a tureen, add a bottle of old Jamaica rum, and five quarts of boiling water; stir well, and serve in glasses.

368. Grog.

Take a quart of boiling tea with half a pound of lump-sugar, and add one pint of Santa Cruz rum or arrack.

369. Holland Punch.

Strain the juice of three or four fine lemons; mix it with one pound of powdered sugar, and one bottle of fine Holland gin; let it stand well covered in a warm place until the sugar is dissolved; add two and a half quarts of boiling water, stir all thoroughly and serve.

370. Hong Kong Punch.

A pound of loaf-sugar in a large enameled pot, the juice of six peeled lemons, the juice of three peeled oranges, one quart of cold water, one bottle of Jamaica rum, half a pint of brandy, one quart bottle of Burgundy; put this over a slow fire, and stir until boiling, then boil about one gallon of mixed tea; mix this all together—hot—and serve. If desired, beat up the whites of three eggs to the form of snow, and use a little of this for the top of each portion. If not sweet enough add sugar to taste.

371. Cold Hoppelpoppel.

The yolks of four eggs and a little ground nutmeg are stirred into half a pint of cold, sweet cream, and beaten to a thick foam; add one gill of Santa Cruz rum, and sweeten to taste.

372. Hot Hoppelpoppel.

One quart of sweet cream and two tablespoonfuls of powdered sugar are heated to the boiling-point; into a little milk stir the yolks of four fresh eggs, and beat all to a thick foam; finally add half a pint of rum.   Serve in glasses or cups.

Instead of cream you may use boiling water or tea.

373. Hot Wine.

Heat one quart of good claret with six ounces of lump-sugar, a stick of cinnamon, six cloves, and the rind of a thinly peeled lemon; let it boil for a moment; strain and serve in glasses.

374. Another.

Boil the rind of a lemon, one-fourth ounce of stick cinnamon, and eight cloves in one pint of water very slowly for half an hour; add two bottles of claret; sweeten all with one pound of lump-sugar; place the well-covered pot in boiling water until the wine boils; strain and serve.

375. Hot Wine à la Française.

Boil three bottles of Bordeaux or Roussillon in an enameled pot with one pound of sugar, one-third ounce of stick cinnamon, two or three leaves of mace, and six bay-leaves; take it from the fire, and light it with a burning paper; let it burn for three minutes, strain, and serve in glasses.

376. Hunters' Punch.

Two bottles of Moselle or light Rhine wine and half a bottle of arrack punch essence are slowly heated in a well-covered enameled pot; heat sufficiently, but avoid boiling; a white, delicious foam will be formed on top, then serve in cut glasses.

377. Iced Punch.

Refine and clear one pound of lump-sugar in one pint of water; let the syrup get cool; add the juice of four or five lemons, and the rind of two rubbed off on sugar; let the mixture freeze in the ice-cream freezer, and add then, while continually turning, a bottle of Rhine wine or champagne, half a pint of Santa Cruz rum or arrack, and half a pony of maraschino; serve the thickly flowing punch in glasses.

378. Imperial Punch.

Peel one pineapple and four oranges; cut the first into small slices, and separate the oranges into pieces; put all in a tureen; then boil in a quart of water two sticks of cinnamon and a stick of vanilla, cut into small pieces; strain the water through a sieve into the tureen; rub the rind of a lemon on one and a half pounds of lump-sugar, put the sugar into the water, and squeeze the juice of three lemons; cover well; let it get cool, place it on ice, add a bottle of Rhine wine, one quart of fine rum, and, shortly before serving, a bottle of champagne and half a bottle of Seltzer.

379. Ladies' Punch.

Put in a tureen the thinly peeled rind and the juice of three blood-oranges, the juice of four lemons with one quart of water; cover, and let it stand for three hours; strain the fluid; add one quart of purified sugar syrup, one quart of brandy, one pint of Santa Cruz rum, and the decoction of half an ounce of stick cinnamon in one and a half quarts of boiling water; heat the punch by placing the tureen in a larger vessel partly filled with water, and serve in glasses.

380. Lemon Punch.

Refine and clear one pound of lump-sugar in one pint of water, and boil it with the rind of a thinly peeled lemon and the juice of three lemons to the consistency of syrup; let it get cool; add three bottles of Rhine wine, three gills of arrack, one pint of light tea; strain through flannel; heat it without boiling, and serve.

381. Another.

Rub the rind of two lemons on half a pound of sugar, add a decoction of one and a half quarts of water and half an ounce of fine tea; squeeze the juice of four lemons; strain; add one pint of old Jamaica rum; heat it once more, and serve.

382. Malinverno Punch.

Clear and refine one pound of sugar in one quart of water; boil one pound of barberries—ripe and well-cleaned—after you have mashed them with a wooden spoon, in the refined sugar syrup; add a bottle of claret, press all through a sieve; add a bottle of Santa Cruz rum, and some raspberry syrup, and you may serve the punch hot or cold.

383. Manhattan Punch.

(HOT OR COLD.)

Take a large enameled pot, the juice of six lemons, the juice of two oranges, a pound of sugar, two quarts of cold water, two quarts of claret, two or three sticks of cinnamon, two dozen cloves, half a pint of Jamaica rum or brandy; place this over a slow fire until boiling; strain carefully before serving. You may serve it hot; if not, you may bottle it, and it will keep for several days.

384. Maraschino Punch.

Three to four bottles of Rhine wine and half a bottle of arrack are mixed with half a bottle of maraschino di Zara and two pounds of cleaned and refined sugar—cold; place the punch for a couple of hours on ice, and add a bottle of champagne just before serving.

385. Maurocordato.

Heat one and a half quarts of sweet cream with a piece of vanilla and half a pound of sugar to the boiling-point; let it then steep for a while; strain the cream through a sieve; beat it with the yolks of six or eight eggs; add enough fine arrack or maraschino to taste.

386. Mecklenburg Punch.

Rub the peel of two lemons on two pounds of sugar; add one and a half quarts of good tea, four bottles of claret, one bottle of French white wine, and one bottle of brandy; let everything get hot over a slow fire; stir well, and serve.

387. Another.

Two pounds of sugar on which two lemons are rubbed off, four bottles of Bordeaux, one bottle of port wine, one bottle of brandy, and half a bottle of Madeira.

388. English Milk Punch.

Rub the peel of three fine lemons on one pound of lump-sugar; put it in a tureen, and squeeze the juice of the fruit over it; grate half a nutmeg; add a bottle of Jamaica rum; mix all thoroughly, and let it stand well covered over night. Then add one quart of boiling water, and one quart of boiling milk; let the mixture stand covered two hours; filter through a canton flannel bag, in which you placed a piece of blotting-paper, until the punch is absolutely clear, and drink it cold.

389. Another.

Rub the peel of two lemons on one and a half pounds of lump-sugar; put this in a tureen; add gradually the juice of the two lemons, a quart of hot milk, one quart of hot water, some pieces of vanilla, cut into small pieces, a little grated nutmeg, and a bottle of good arrack, and let the well-covered tureen stand over night. The following morning you filter the thick fluid through a flannel bag, until it gets clear; fill into bottles, and serve the punch cold; it may be kept as long as you please.

390. Another.

In a bottle of fine rum put the thinly peeled rind of three oranges and three lemons; cork the bottle well, and let the bottle stand two days. After this rub the rind of six lemons on two pounds of loaf-sugar, squeeze their juice and that of the formerly peeled lemons and oranges over the sugar; add two quarts of boiling water, one and a half quarts of boiling milk, and half a teaspoonful of grated nutmeg, and mix all well until the sugar is dissolved. Now add the rum; strain the punch until it is perfectly clear; fill into bottles, and cork them very well.

Such a milk-punch is a beverage refreshing and harmless, which, in summer especially, for excursions, picnics, etc., cannot be too highly appreciated.

391. Finland Milk Punch.

This punch is prepared like our first "English Milk Punch;" only take Santa Cruz rum instead of Jamaica rum, and leave the nutmeg out.

392. Warm Milk Punch.

A quart of fresh milk is slowly heated to boiling with the thin peel of a small lemon; then strain the milk, beat it with the yolks of four eggs, stirred up beforehand in cold milk; add a wineglass-ful of brandy, and two wineglassfuls of rum; beat all over a slow fire to foam, and fill into glasses.

393. Nectar Punch à l'Amérique.

(FOR BOTTLING.)

Infuse the rind of fifteen thinly peeled lemons forty-eight hours in one and a half pints of rum; filter; add two quarts of cold water and three pints of rum, the juice of the lemons, a grated nutmeg, and two and a half quarts of boiling milk; cover well, let stand for twenty-four hours, and sweeten with three pounds of sugar; strain through a flannel bag, until the punch is perfectly clear, and bottle.

394. Negus.

This beverage is of English origin, and there very highly estimated; it derives its name from its inventor, the English Colonel Negus.

Put the rind of half a lemon or orange in a tureen, add eight ounces of sugar, one pint of port wine, the fourth part of a small nutmeg—grated; infuse this for an hour; strain; add one quart of boiling water, and the drink is ready for use.

395. Another.

In other countries they are used to take lighter wines. The recipe follows: Put two bottles of claret, two sticks of cinnamon, six cloves, a little pulverized cardamom, a little grated nutmeg, and half a pound of sugar, on which you have previously rubbed the rind of a lemon, on a slow fire; cover well, and heat to the boiling-point; strain through a hair-sieve; add one pint of boiling water, and the juice of one and a half lemons, and serve in strong glasses, that are first warmed.

396. Norfolk Punch.

Infuse the rind of fifteen lemons and of as many oranges, thinly peeled, in two quarts of brandy or rum for forty-eight hours; filter the infusion, and add it to the cold syrup of two pounds of sugar and two and a half quarts of water; squeeze the juice of the lemons and oranges; pour all into a great stone jug, tie with a bladder, and let it stand for from six to eight weeks before using.

397. Nuremberg Punch.

Rub lightly the peel of an orange on three-fourths pound of sugar; squeeze the juice of two oranges on it; pour one quart of boiling water over it; add a small pint of good old arrack, and a bottle of old Bordeaux—hot, but not boiling; mix all well, and serve.

398. Orange Punch.

Rub the peel of three oranges on sugar; place the sugar in a pot; add the juice of six oranges and two lemons, one pound of lump-sugar, one bottle of white wine, one quart of water; let all boil; pour it into a bowl, and add two bottles of white wine, and one and a half pints of arrack or rum.

399. Prince of Wales Punch.
(COLD.)

In a small bowl put the thinly peeled and cut rind of half a lemon, and two and a half ounces of granulated sugar; add one-fourth quart of boiling water; let it stand for a quarter of an hour; add a bottle of champagne, and a gill of the best arrack; mix the fluids well, and place the bowl on ice one or two hours.

400. Port Wine Punch.

A bottle of claret, a bottle of Rhine wine, and a bottle of port wine are heated with two pounds of sugar, until the sugar is dissolved; do not let it boil; meanwhile squeeze the juice of four lemons into a tureen, add half a bottle of fine arrack and the sweet mixture; stir well, and serve.

401. Punch à la Diable.

Place on the stove a large enameled pot, in which, before, water had been boiling; lay on it two flat iron bars, and place on these two pounds of lump-sugar; pour over the sugar a bottle of old Jamaica rum, and light it carefully with a burning paper, to let the melting sugar flow into the pot; when the flame goes out by itself, add three bottles of Rhine wine, and one quart of black tea, the juice of one lemon and of one orange; let it stand covered three hours in a warm, but not hot oven.

402. Punch à l'Empereur.

Rub on three pounds of lump-sugar the rind of one orange
and one lemon; squeeze the juice of four lemons on the sugar;
boil in one and a half quarts of water, until it becomes clear;
add half a bottle of arrack, one bottle of Rhine wine, and one
bottle of Burgundy, and let the punch simmer for a while without letting it boil; then serve.

403. Punch à la Crême.

Dissolve four pounds of sugar in four quarts of hot water;
heat this with four quarts of arrack, the juice of eight lemons, and
a small piece of vanilla, cut in pieces, in an enameled pot to the
boiling-point; as soon as this is reached add three quarts of milk
or cream, while constantly stirring. Take the vessel from the
fire, tie a cloth over it, let it stand for two hours; filter, bottle,
and keep it for future use, as it may be preserved for a very long
time.

404. Punch à la Bavaroise.

Rub the rind of three lemons on one pound of lump-sugar;
squeeze the juice of the fruit on it; add one quart of water and
two bottles of Burgundy; heat slowly to the boiling-point; filter
through canton flannel, and serve it hot.

405. Punch à la Ford.

Three dozen lemons are very thinly peeled; the rind is put
in an enameled pot, three pounds of sugar added, and all is stirred for about half an hour; add five quarts of boiling water; stir
until the sugar is dissolved; add to each three quarts one pint of
the best Jamaica rum and one pint of brandy; bottle the punch,
keep it in the cellar, and use it after the expiration of some weeks
—the later the better.

406. Punch à la Française.

Put one and a half pounds of lump-sugar in a new earthen pot, pour over it one quart of rum; light this, and let burn until the sugar becomes brown and is melted to one-third of its original volume; add three-fourths quart of boiling tea, the juice of six lemons and of six oranges; stir well, and serve at once.

407. Another.

Two pounds of sugar in an earthen pot are mixed with half a glass of water or tea, the juice of two lemons and two oranges, and cleared and refined to syrup; add a bottle of rum, a bottle of brandy, and tea, until the punch receives the required mildness. Heat, and, before serving, squeeze the juice of six oranges through a sieve.

408. Punch à la Régence.

The thinly peeled rind of two lemons and two bitter oranges are put in a tureen with some vanilla, and as much cinnamon, and four cloves, poured over with the boiling syrup of one and a half pounds of sugar and three-fourths quart of water, and placed aside for two hours. Add the purified juice of twelve lemons, one bottle of old Jamaica rum, and half a bottle of brandy; filter the punch through a cloth, fill into bottles, and place the bottles on ice.

409. Punch à la Reine.

Rub the rind of two or three lemons off on one-fourth pound of sugar, squeeze the juice of six lemons and two oranges on it; add a syrup of three-fourths pound of sugar and three gills of water; after all is well mixed let it freeze in the freezing-can; mix a cup of rum and as much brandy to the ice, likewise the thick foam of the whites of three eggs, sweetened with vanilla-sugar; leave the punch for a while in the freezing-can, and serve.

410. Punch à la Romaine.

Rub the rind of two oranges and one lemon on one and a half pounds of sugar; put it in a tureen, and add one pint of water; when the sugar is properly dissolved add the juice of four oranges and two lemons, half a bottle of Rhine wine, half a pint of arrack, half a pint of maraschino, and a pint-bottle of champagne; place the mixture in the freezing-can, turn continually, and let it freeze; finally, stir the froth of the whites of five eggs, sweetened with sugar, to it; let all freeze for a while, until it looks like thick cream; serve in champagne glasses.

411. Another.

Rub the peel of six lemons off on sugar; squeeze the juice of the lemons and of two oranges; add half a pint of water and one pint of sugar-syrup out of three-fourths pound of sugar and one pint of water; stir all well, and let it freeze in the freezing-can. Then mix the solid froth of the whites of four eggs with half a pound of pulverized sugar; add this, with three gills of brandy, a bottle of champagne, and a cup of green tea, to the ice; mix all thoroughly; leave the punch for a short while in the freezing-can, and serve in glasses.

412. Punch à la Tyrolienne.

The thin peel of four lemons, half an ounce of stick cinnamon, six cloves, two pounds of sugar, one and a half quarts of water are heated over a slow fire until the sugar is dissolved. Add the juice of eight lemons, two quarts of claret, one bottle of arrack, one quart of white wine; heat it once more to the boiling-point, and serve.

413. Raspberry Punch.

Two quarts of moderately strong black tea are mixed with one pint of raspberry-juice, and heated; then dissolve in it two pounds of sugar; let the fluid boil for a few seconds; add one quart of arrack de Batavia, and serve at once.

414. Another.

Add to half a pint of raspberry syrup three and one-half pints of boiling water, half a pint of Santa Cruz rum, and half a pint of brandy; sweeten to taste; add a pony of maraschino; stir well, and serve.

415. Rhine Wine Punch.

Heat three bottles of Rhine wine nearly to boiling; add one quart of strong tea, twelve ounces of sugar on which you have rubbed the rind of a lemon, the juice of the lemon, and one or two gills of fine arrack; mix all well, and serve.

416. Another.

Heat very slowly six bottles of Rhine wine, three-fourths quart of old Jamaica rum, one and three-fourths to two pounds of sugar nearly to the boiling-point, and serve hot.

417. Royal Punch.

Three pounds of lump-sugar are put in a tureen, then pour over it one quart of light hot tea—as soon as the sugar is perfectly dissolved squeeze in the juice of three lemons and three oranges; add one pint of fine Rhine wine, as much Bordeaux. champagne, arrack, maraschino, and pineapple syrup; mix all very well, and place the tureen, well covered, on ice.

418. Rum Punch.

Put two pounds of sugar in a tureen; squeeze on it the juice of five lemons, add the thin peel of two lemons, and three quarts of boiling water. After the sugar is dissolved add a bottle of old Jamaica rum, and a bottle of champagne, and serve cold or hot.

419. Russian Punch.

Rub the peel of four lemons and of four oranges off on two pounds of sugar; put it in a tureen; add the juice of the fruits, and one and a half quarts of cold water; let the tureen stand until the sugar is melted; fill all in a freezing-can, and prepare ice-cream of it. Then add gradually one bottle of champagne, and half a bottle of arrack; mix all well, and serve in glasses.

420. Sapazeau.

Rub the yellow rind of four fine oranges lightly on half a pound of loaf-sugar; pulverize; put in a kettle; squeeze the juice of the fruit on it; add six eggs, and the yolks of four; beat them well; add one and a half quarts of Rhine wine, and beat all over a slow fire to a thick, boiling mass. Take the Sapazeau from the fire, mix with a small cup of maraschino, and serve hot in cups or glass mugs.

421. Snow-Flakes.

Two bottles of Moselle or Rhine wine are slowly heated with some lemon-peel and four ounces of sugar. Beat the whites of four eggs with a little powdered sugar and some lemon extract to a thick foam; with a spoon take off small snowballs from the foam, and place them in the boiling wine; take them out again carefully with a lifter; then stir the yolks of the eggs in a little wine, and add it to the hot wine while continually stirring. Pour the wine in a bowl; place the snowballs on top, and grate a little cinnamon.

422. Sporting Punch.

A bottle of brandy, half a pint of Jamaica rum, half a pint of peach brandy, a wineglassful of curaçao, one-fourth pound of sugar—dissolved in hot water; mix all this in a bowl; add a lump of ice, and serve.

423. Steel Punch.

Infuse a small stick of vanilla, some stick cinnamon, and two cloves in half a pint of water on a warm place, about 200° F., well covered; filter into an enameled pot; add one quart of claret, five ounces of powdered sugar, and stir very well; make an iron red hot, hold it in the fluid until it gets cold; stir the yolks of six eggs in a little claret, add them, and beat all to foam over a slow fire.

424. Strawberry Punch.

Two quarts of fine, ripe strawberries are mashed in a stone pot; add one bottle of Santa Cruz rum; tie it closely, and let it stand three days; stir once a day; strain and squeeze through canton flannel; now put one pound of granulated sugar in a bowl; press the juice of two lemons thereon; pour the rum over it, and add finally three quarts of boiling water; cover the bowl well, and do not serve before the punch is perfectly cold.

425. "Texas Siftings" Punch.

Pare off the peel of four blood-oranges very thin; pour over it a large glass of white wine; let soak for half a day in a well-covered tureen; strain the wine into a bowl; add two bottles of good Bordeaux, two bottles of Rhine or Moselle wine, and two bottles of champagne; sweeten to taste; mix all well, and serve in glasses.

426. Uhles.

A bottle of white wine, as much water, and four ounces of sugar are heated to the boiling-point; the yolks of six eggs beaten into it to a thick foam, mixed with two wineglassfuls of arrack; serve in glass mugs.

427. United Service Punch.

In one and a fourth quarts of hot, strong tea dissolve one pound of sugar; add the juice of six lemons, one pint of arrack, and one pint of port wine; warm up, and serve.

428. Vin Brulé.

Two bottles of white wine with three-fourths pound of sugar, on which the peel of two lemons was rubbed off, the juice of the lemons, and a piece of cinnamon are placed over a slow fire in a well-covered new earthen pot; just before boiling add, through a hair-sieve, the yolks of eight or ten eggs, beaten in a little wine; take it from the fire, and serve in glasses.

429. Washington's Punch.

The juice of six lemons in a large bowl, a pound of sugar, a pint of Jamaica rum, a pint of brandy, one and a half pints of black tea; add five or six bottles of champagne; mix this well; add some sliced oranges and pineapples, one large piece of ice, and serve.

430. Whiskey Punch.

Rub the rind of three lemons on seven ounces of sugar; put the sugar in a tureen; add one quart of boiling water and the juice of the fruit; this syrup is mixed with one pint or more of old Irish whiskey.

431. Whist.

Half an ounce of Pecco tea is infused in one pint of boiling water; pour the tea through a hair-sieve upon one pound of sugar; squeeze the juice of five or six lemons, and mix all with three quarts of very good Bordeaux; heat without boiling, and serve in glasses.

Bowls.

432. Ananas Bowl.

Peel a fresh pineapple, cut it into slices; place that in a large bowl, and cover with one pound of pulverized sugar; cover the bowl well, and let it stand from twelve to twenty-four hours; add, according to the number of guests, three, four, or more bottles of Rhine wine; for every bottle of wine add six ounces of lump-sugar; place on ice, and add, before serving, a bottle of champagne.

433. Ananas Cardinal.

Peel a fresh pineapple; cut it into slices; put that in a bowl, sugar it well, pour in one bottle of Rhine wine, and let it stand for a couple of hours; add, then, according to the number of guests, three or four bottles of Rhine wine; put it on ice, and serve.

434. Ananas Julep.

Peel a ripe pineapple; cut it into thin slices, and place that in a bowl; add the juice of two oranges, one gill of raspberry syrup, one gill of maraschino, one gill of old Holland gin, one bottle of sparkling Moselle wine, and a scoop of shaved ice; mix thoroughly, and fill into glasses.

435. Apple Bowl.

Peel twelve good, juicy, aromatic apples; remove the seeds; cut them into thin slices; put in a tureen thickly strewed with fine sugar; cover the tureen well, and let it stand in a cool place twenty-four hours; add a wineglassful of old Jamaica rum, and let it stand again for two hours; pour three to four bottles of a light Moselle or Rhine wine over it; put the tureen on ice for a few hours; strain the wine through flannel, and add one bottle of champagne.

436. Badminton.

Peel one-half of a cucumber of medium size; cut into rather thick slices; put them in a bowl; add six ounces of pulverized sugar; grate a little nutmeg on top of it, and add a bottle of claret; put the bowl on ice, and add, after stirring, a siphon of Seltzer.

437. English Beer Bowl.

Infuse the peel of a lemon, a thin slice of toast, some ground nutmeg and some pulverized ginger in a large wineglassful of brandy; add a sprig of borage, one of pimpernel, and some slices of peeled apples; pour over it two quarts of porter or ale, sweeten with three tablespoonfuls of sugar; cool it, and serve with cheese, bread and butter.

438. Cold Bishop.

Peel a green, bitter orange very thin; put that in a new earthen pot; infuse it in one bottle of best Bordeaux or Burgundy in the well-covered pot from ten to twelve hours; strain, and sweeten at discretion.

439. English Bishop.

(WARM.)

Make slight incisions into the rind of four small, bitter oranges; roast them before a fire, on a grate, on both sides; place them in an enameled pot; add two bottles of fine claret, a few pieces of cinnamon and a fried bread-crust; cover the pot well, and let it simmer from six to eight hours; strain the wine through flannel, and sweeten to taste and serve.

440. Russian Bishop.

Peel the rind of four bitter oranges; put in a tureen and infuse with three bottles of Muscat Lunel for an hour; strain the wine through flannel; bottle, and place on ice for one or two hours; then serve in glasses.

441. Cardinal.

Peel four bitter oranges with a sharp knife, very carefully; infuse the peel with four bottles of Rhine wine for ten hours; sweeten with one and a half pounds of sugar; put it on ice; strain and serve.

442. Another.

Take two bitter and two sweet oranges; rub the rind of them on one and a half pounds of lump-sugar; put the sugar in a bowl; press the juice of the two sweet oranges over it; add a bottle of white wine; put it on ice; strain and serve.

443. Another.

Peel three small oranges; put the rind in a bowl and pour a bottle of Moselle wine over it; strain the wine after eight hours; press the juice of seven or eight oranges on two pounds of lump-sugar; let the sugar melt in the first bottle of Moselle wine; add three others and a bottle of port wine; a little ananas syrup will increase exceedingly the taste of the bowl.

444. Celery Bowl à l'Amérique.

Peel three or four fresh celery-roots; cut them into thin slices; cover them in a bowl thickly with powdered sugar; infuse with half a bottle of brandy, arrack, or rum, well covered, for twelve hours; strain, and add four bottles of Rhine wine and one bottle of champagne; put it for two hours on ice, and add, before serving, a scoop of fine ice.

445. English Cider Bowl.

Make an extract of a spoonful of green tea in a half-pint of boiling water; let it stand for fifteen minutes; pour it into a bowl; add six ounces of lump-sugar, one bottle of cider, two wineglassfuls of brandy, half a pint of cold water, a couple of fresh cucumber slices, some leaves of borage, and two leaves of Roman sage, and place the bowl on ice.

446. Another.

Peel a lemon or orange very thin; infuse the rind in a cup of boiling water in a bowl; add some borage-leaves, some cucumber slices, some sprigs of balm, half a pound of sugar, one pint of sherry, Madeira or Malaga (or, instead of this, two wineglassfuls of brandy), and two bottles of cider; put the bowl on ice and serve.

447. Champagne Bowl.

To one pound of lump-sugar add two bottles of Moselle wine, one bottle of Burgundy and two bottles of champagne; cover the bowl well and put it on ice.

448. Sherry Bowl.

The rind of six lemons is infused four hours in one-fourth quart of boiling water; pour this water in a bowl; add the juice of two lemons, one pint of sherry, three gills of old Jamaica rum, three gills of brandy, one pound of lump-sugar, three pints of cold water, and one pint of boiling milk; mix everything thoroughly; strain it through flannel, and put it for four hours on ice.

449. English Claret Bowl.

Peel an orange and cut it in slices, likewise half a cucumber; add a few sprigs of borage and balm, two or three tablespoonfuls of pulverized sugar, a wineglassful of brandy, or two glasses of sherry, two bottles of claret, and a bottle of Seltzer; stir everything well, put it two hours on ice, and strain before serving.

450. English Gin Bowl.

Put the rind of a thinly peeled lemon and its juice in a tureen, add three tablespoonfuls of powdered sugar, and one quart of water, and let it stand an hour; pour over it one pint of Old Tom gin, a wineglassful of maraschino, three tablespoonfuls of shaved ice, and a bottle of Seltzer, and serve.

451. Hippocras.

A kind of spiced wine of the mediæval age, when one did
not yet understand blending the wines, consequently they always
were of a certain acidity, which was covered by addition of honey
and spices. A recipe for manufacturing hippocras, which Talley-
raut, the head cook of Charles VII., king of France, has made,
reads as follows: To a quart of wine take one-third of an ounce
of very fine and clean cinnamon, one-thirtieth ounce of ginger,
twice as much of cloves, as much of nutmeg, and six ounces of
sugar and honey; grind the spices, put them in a muslin bag,
hang this in the wine for ten to twelve hours, and filter several
times.

Wherever, nowadays, hippocras is made, it is made in the following manner: Cut eight to ten large, aromatic, well-peeled
apples into thin slices; put that in a tureen, add half a pound of
sugar, three or four pepper kernels, the rind of a lemon, one-
third of an ounce of whole cinnamon, two ounces of peeled and
mashed almonds, and four cloves; pour over this two bottles of
Rhine wine, cover it well, and let it soak with the other ingredients; filter the wine, and you may use this wine also for a bowl.

452. Linden Blossom Bowl.

Pluck fully developed linden blossoms; look carefully that no
insects are on them; put them in a tureen; pour over that two
bottles of Rhine wine; cover the tureen well, and let it stand from
six to eight hours; strain, and add wine according to the number of guests; sweeten to taste, and add finally a pint bottle of
champagne or a bottle of Seltzer.

453. May Bowl.

For the preparation of this favorite spring beverage there is
a number of more or less complicated recipes, of which we first
give the simplest one, and afterwards some of the more complicated ones.

Put a handful of woodruff (*asperula odorata*) that has no
blossoms yet, in a bowl; pour over it two bottles of Moselle wine,
cover the bowl, let it soak not longer than half an hour in a very

cool place; take the woodruff out, sweeten with from four to five ounces of sugar, stir well, and serve the aromatic beverage at once. You improve the fine taste by adding the thin slices of one or two peeled oranges. If you prepare this delicious beverage in this simple way, it is the best, as the unadulterated aroma of the woodruff is obtained; but take care that you do not leave the herb too long in the wine or you will get headache from it.

454. Another.

Two handfuls of woodruff, two or three oranges cut into slices, two bottles of white wine, and two bottles of claret are put in a bowl; let it infuse an hour, take the herb out, and sweeten to taste.

455. Another.

A handful of woodruff, four sprigs of balm, four to six mint-leaves, as many young strawberry-leaves, and cassis-leaves are put in a bowl; add two lemons cut into slices, freed from peel and seeds, and two or three bottles of Moselle wine; let soak not longer than half an hour, add sugar to taste, and ice, if desired.

(*N. B.* The first one is, to repeat it once more, the simplest and best one.)

456. Militia Bowl.

A beverage similar to Bishop or Cardinal. Infuse the rind of two lemons in one quart of good, white wine six or eight hours; filter the wine, sweeten with half a pound of sugar, put it on ice, and use it when you please.

457. Nectar.

Peel twelve ripe, very fine choice apples; cut into very thin slices; put that in a bowl with the thinly peeled rind of two lemons, cover the slices thickly with powdered sugar, and pour over it a bottle of Rhine or Moselle wine. Cover the bowl, and let it stand from ten to fourteen hours; add, the following day, a bottle of Moselle and one of champagne; put the bowl on ice, and serve.

458. Nectar in the English Style.

(FOR BOTTLING.)

Put the rind of two or three lemons, one pound of raisins (without seeds and cut in pieces), one and a half pounds of loaf-sugar, in a tureen, and pour over it nine quarts of boiling water; after cooling add the juice of the lemons, let the beverage stand a week in a cool place; stir daily, then filter through a flannel bag, and bottle; you may use it right away.

459. Another.

Two pounds of raisins (without seeds and cut in small pieces) and four pounds of sugar are infused in nine quarts of boiling water; stir until the water is getting cool; add two lemons (cut in slices), one and a half to two quarts of rum or best brandy; cover the vessel well and let it stand a week; stir daily a few times, press all through flannel, let it stand for another week for getting clear; decant into bottles for immediate or future use.

460. Orange Bowl.

Rub the peel of one large or two small oranges on sugar; pour over it a bottle of Moselle wine, and let it stand two hours; then peel six oranges very neatly, divide them into nice cuts, remove the seeds and their inner skin, partially, that the juice may flow out freely; add one pound of pulverized sugar and four bottles of white wine; put the bowl on ice, and add, before serving, a bottle of champagne.

461. Orange Cardinal.

Peel an orange very thin with a sharp knife; add three bottles of Rhine wine; let it stand at least from eight to twelve hours; strain the wine through a sieve; add the juice of six oranges and one and a half pounds of sugar.

462. Orgeat.

This is a cooling beverage, especially adapted for sick persons who are forbidden to drink lemonades; but in many cases, as by dancing parties, musical entertainments, etc., also for the healthy, very refreshing and pleasing.

Pour boiling water over one-fourth pound of sweet and eight to ten bitter almonds; place in a sieve; skin them; mash with one-fourth of a pound of sugar, and add, while mashing, a few drops of cold water. Put it in a china pot; add, gradually, one pint of cold water, stir well, and let the mixture stand in a cool place two hours; strain through a cloth; place it on ice; add another quart of cold water and one pony of orange-flower water, and serve.

463. Peach Bowl.

Peel ten to twelve peaches; cut them in quarters; remove the seeds; put that in a bowl; strew thickly with powdered sugar, cover the bowl well, and let it stand from eight to ten hours; add two bottles of Rhine or Moselle wine; place the bowl on ice, and add, finally, a bottle of Seltzer or of champagne.

464. The Pope.

A bowl similar to Bishop or Cardinal, only use Tokay wine instead of red and white wine.

Pare off the rind of two small bitter oranges; put the rind in a bottle of Tokay; cork well, and let stand for twenty-four hours; filter, and sweeten to taste.

465. English Porter Bowl.

Cut three lemons into thin slices; remove the seeds; put the slices in a bowl; pour over it half a pint of sherry and one quart of porter; grate a little nutmeg; place on ice and serve.

466. Bowl à la Parisienne.

(FOR TWELVE.)

A large bowl, containing about two gallons; the juice of six peeled lemons, the juice of six peeled oranges, one pound of pulverized sugar, two quarts of champagne, two quarts of Burgundy; dissolve this exceedingly well; add a bottle of Jamaica rum, half a bottle of brandy, a whiskey-tumbler of chartreuse (green or yellow), three ponies of benedictine, two ponies of curaçao, two ponies of maraschino, one bottle of plain soda, or other mineral water. You may add a small pineapple, peeled and sliced. Mix this well, and have it cold on a large piece of ice; serve in fine glasses.

467. Raspberry Bowl.

The same recipe as for a strawberry bowl, only raspberries in-instead of strawberries.

468. Réséda Bowl.

On a dry, sunny day pluck a little basket of fully developed mignonette blossoms; free them from all green leaves; cut the stalks off to the blossoms, and look carefully that no insects or small caterpillars are on them; then place them in a tureen; infuse them for twelve hours, well covered in half a pint of arrack or brandy and half a bottle of Rhine wine; strain through flannel; add three bottles of Rhine wine; sweeten to taste; put it on ice, and add, before serving, a bottle of champagne or Seltzer.

469. Rum Flip.

Heat three-fourths of a pint of ale; beat three or four eggs with four ounces of pulverized sugar, a teaspoonful of pulverized ginger, a little grated nutmeg and a finely chopped lemon-peel and a gill of old Jamaica rum to a consistent foam; add the nearly boiling ale, while constantly stirring, and pour the beverage a few times from one vessel into another; serve in glasses.

470. Sillabub.

This word is derived from the old English words, "to sile" ("to strain,") "and "bub" ("beverage").

In a large china pot mix one pint of rich, sweet cream, one pint of good Rhine or Hungarian wine, four or five ounces of sugar, on which you have rubbed off the rind of a lemon and the juice of a lemon; let it get very cold on ice; beat to a thick foam, and serve in glasses or cups as dessert, or after coffee.

471. Red Sillabub.

On half a pound of sugar rub the rind of two lemons; break the sugar and dissolve it in a quart of sweet cream; mix three-fourths of a quart of claret and the juice of the lemons with the cream; place on ice for an hour, and serve.

472. Strawberry Bowl.

Take one pint of choice strawberries; cover them with powdered sugar; then take three pints of strawberries and infuse them with one pint of hot sugar syrup two hours; strain them through flannel upon the sugared strawberries; add three or four bottles of Moselle wine; put the bowl on ice, and add, finally, a bottle of champagne.

473. Sweet Bowl.

One pound of powdered sugar, one and a half lemons cut in slices, without the seeds, and one-fourth of an ounce of stick cinnamon, are infused in a bottle of Moselle or Rhine wine twelve hours; strain and serve in glasses.

474. West Indian Sangaree.

Pulverize one-fourth of a pound of loaf-sugar; add one wine-glassful of lemon or lime juice; stir well; add a bottle of Madeira, half a pint of good brandy, and one quart of cold water; mix all well, and grate the fourth part of a little nutmeg on top; put in a big lump of ice, and serve with biscuits.

This is a favorite drink in the West Indies, and usually taken cold.

Kaltschalen.

475. Apple Bishop.

Peel eighteen to twenty fine, aromatic apples; cut them into thin slices, steam one-third of them with seven ounces of raisins, one glass of Rhine wine, seven ounces of sugar, and the juice of a lemon, and put on ice. The rest of the apple slices are boiled in one and a half quarts of water with some lemon-peel and stick cinnamon to a mash; strain; mix with a bottle of Rhine wine and one pound of pulverized sugar, and serve over the steamed apple slices on plates.

476. Apricot Bishop.

Peel about twelve fine, soft apricots; four of them are cut in pieces and boiled with the skinned seeds (chopped) and with the peel of the apricots and half a pound of sugar; boil half an hour well, strain through a sieve upon the others, which you have cut in two; let all get cold, and add a few glasses of white wine.

477. Beer Bishop.

Pumpernickel is grated on a grater and put in a tureen; mix with it one-fourth of a pound of powdered sugar, one-fourth of a pound of choice raisins, a teaspoonful of powdered cinnamon, an unpeeled lemon, cut in pieces without seeds; add a quart of white beer or lager (*Franziskaner*), and serve.

478. Bilberry Bishop.

Boil two quarts of well-cleaned bilberries with half a pint of water, one-fourth of a pound of sugar, some lemon-peel and some stick cinnamon; strain through a sieve, mix it with two quarts of white wine, cream or milk, place the mixture on ice, and serve over broken Zwieback, grated pumpernickel or snow-balls.

479. Cherry Bishop.

Remove the pits of one and a half quarts of fine sour cherries, break one part of the pits, put the cherries and pits with one pint of wine, one and a half quarts of water, six ounces of sugar, some stick cinnamon and lemon-peel in a tureen; let all boil thoroughly until the cherries are perfectly soft; then stir a table-spoonful of corn-starch in cold water, mix that, while continually stirring, to the cherries, let boil a while, strain all through a hair-sieve, and put on ice. When serving, add broken Zwieback, cherries steamed in wine and sugar, snowballs of the beaten whites of eggs, seasoned with lemon sugar, etc.

480. Currant Bishop.

One quart of choice currants are strained through a hair-sieve and mixed with half a pound of powdered sugar and a good quart of light, white wine; put on ice and serve over broken Zwieback or small biscuits.

481. Lemon Bishop.

A bottle of white wine with one quart of water and nine ounces of sugar are heated to the boiling-point (without boiling); add the yolks of six eggs and a spoonful of flour well whipped, and take it from the fire; strain through a sieve, add the peel of two lemons, which you rubbed off on half a pound of sugar, and their juice; mix well and let it get cold in the cellar. When serving, add some biscuits or macaroni.

482. Melon Bishop.

A half or whole very ripe melon is cut into small, cubic pieces; cover them well with sugar, squeeze over it the juice of a lemon and let soak for an hour; add two or three bottles of light, ice-cold white wine; stir thoroughly, add some small biscuits and serve.

483. Mulberry Bishop.

Select from one pint of ripe mulberries the third or fourth part, *i. e.*, the largest and best, place the rest in one or one and a half quarts of water over a slow fire and boil them well; strain, add one pint of wine (best red wine), some lemon-peel and seven ounces of sugar; boil this well together, let it get cold, and serve over the selected berries which you covered with sugar.

484. Orange Bishop.

On half a pound of sugar rub the rind of two oranges; heat to the boiling-point in one pint of water; when the water has got cold, squeeze the juice of four oranges, add one bottle of white wine and the peeled slices of two oranges.

485. Peach Bishop.

Boil a number of peaches cut in two, soft in water after you have removed their pits; mix them with one and a half quarts of white wine and three-fourths of a pound of sugar and let it get cold on ice.

486. Pineapple Bishop.

Peel a pineapple and cut into four pieces; one-half is cut into slices; cover these with sugar and place on ice; grate the other half, boil it up in one quart of sugar syrup and press through a cloth; add to this syrup one and a half bottles of Rhine wine and the juice of a lemon, sweeten to taste with powdered sugar, put wine and slices in a tureen, let it get cold on ice and serve in glasses or on plates.

487. Raspberry Bishop.

From one quart of choice raspberries select the best, cover them with sugar in a tureen, then press the remaining berries through a hair-sieve, mix with one pint of water, one bottle of white wine, the rind of a lemon rubbed off on eight ounces of sugar; pour this mixture over the berries in the tureen, let it get cold on ice and serve with small biscuits.

488. Rice with Wine.

Rub the rind of a lemon on a little over half a pound of sugar; refine this in three-fourths of a quart of water, let it cool, add one bottle of white wine and the juice of two lemons and one-fourth of a pound of rice, slowly boiled before, and place all on ice.

489. Strawberry Bishop.

Put one quart of choice strawberries in a tureen and let it stand with six ounces of powdered sugar an hour; add one quart of white wine, as much of water, and the juice of a lemon; sweeten to taste and grate a little cinnamon on it.

Extra Drinks.

490. Champagne Beer.

Boil in a large, very clean earthen pot five gallons of water with one and a half pounds of sugar—brown rock-candy is the best—until the sugar is completely dissolved; when the water is cool add one and three-fourths ounces of yeast; stir well; cover the pot, and let it stand over night. The following day take off the yeast on the top; place the fluid in a cool place, and decant it into another vessel very carefully; add a stick of cinnamon, and one ounce of lump-sugar, which has been moistened with twelve drops of lemon-oil; let it stand for a couple of hours; bottle and cork well, and put it in the cellar; you may use it after four or five days.

491. Egg Beer.

Place one quart of beer with four ounces of sugar, a stick of cinnamon, and some pieces of lemon-peel in a pot over the fire, and heat it to boiling; meanwhile beat six whole fresh eggs to foam, and add the boiling beer, while continually stirring; then serve it in cups.

492. Ginger Beer.

Put in a large earthen vessel the rind of a thinly peeled lemon and the juice of four, two ounces of pulverized ginger, two and one-half pounds of powdered sugar, half an ounce of cremor tartari; pour over it ten quarts of boiling water, and add, after the water is lukewarm only, one ounce of pressed yeast, dissolved in a little water; stir the fluid well, and let it ferment to the following day. Then take off the yeast on top; decant the beer carefully into bottles, so as not to disturb the yeast; cork well, and the beer is ready for use after three or four days.

493. Ginger Pop.

Put one pound of lump-sugar, one ounce of pulverized ginger, one ounce of cremor tartari in five quarts of boiling water; when the water is nearly cold, add one ounce of pressed yeast, dissolved in a little water; strain it into bottles; tie the cork with wire, and you may use the beverage after six or eight hours.

494. Gloria.

The French are very fond of this beverage.

Take very strong, well-strained coffee, and pour it over half a cupful of sugar; the result will be a consistent syrup; in the moment of serving pour in a teaspoonful of brandy; light it, and extinguish the flame after a few seconds, and drink the gloria as hot as you possibly can.

495. Kvass.

This, for every Russian household, necessary national beverage, which is also used for different soups and other dishes, is manufactured for the family use in the following way:

Ten pounds of rye flour, one pound of malt, and one pound of buckwheat flour are stirred in a tub with three quarts of warm water; then pour over it three quarts of boiling water; after half an hour add again six quarts of boiling water, and repeat this in half-hourly intervals three times more; stir the flour in the water well; let it get cool, cover, and let it stand in a rather warm place; the following day you thin the kvass with cold water; put it in a cool place; let it thoroughly sour, and bottle. When the kvass is nearly used up, leave a couple of quarts of the beverage in the tub for the next souring; the thick sediment at the bottom is then thrown away, but it may be used on farms successfully as food for the beasts of burden.

Another recipe is the following:

Twenty pounds of rye flour, and as much malt flour are stirred with cold water, and kneaded well; then form loaves of bread from ten to twelve pounds each; press with the fingers some deep holes into them; pour cold water into these holes; place the loaves in a very hot baking-oven, and bake them brownish black; leave them over night in the oven; break forty pounds to moderate-sized pieces; put them in a tub; pour fifty to sixty quarts of boiling water over them; cover the pot with canton flannel and a wooden lid very well, and let soak for two hours. Pour the entire quantity into a cask, the bottom of which is covered with cross-laid slats, which again are covered by straw to prevent the falling through of the bread; through a side-faucet decant the kvass, and fill it again into the cask; repeat this a few times to clear it sufficiently; in a vessel already soured it need stay for only twenty-four hours, but in a new cask it must stand for a few days until it is sufficiently sour.

Besides this bread-kvass, this beverage may be made also from fruits: so you may make apple-kvass by rowing apple-slices and whole pears on strings, and drying them in the sun; in a cask of about fifteen gallons you put twenty-four quarts of dried apples, and as many dried pears, and fill the cask with boiled but cooled-off water; let it stand for three days on a rather warm place; then bring it into the cellar; cover the bung-hole with canvas, and let the kvass ferment. After fermentation bung the cask; bottle after four weeks; add to each bottle a handful of raisins; cork, and seal, and let them lie a few months in a cellar; cover them with a layer of sand.

Fruit Wines.

496. English Apricot Wine.

Boil twelve pounds of ripe, stoneless apricots with one pound of lump-sugar, half an hour, in twelve quarts of water; add one-fourth of the peeled and roughly mashed kernels, and let the fluid get cool in a well-covered vessel. After cooling, add, while stirring, a tablespoonful of beer-yeast; let it ferment three or four days. Then fill the juice into a very well-cleaned cask, and add, when the fermentation is complete, a bottle of Rhine wine; let the cask rest for half a year, fill the contents into bottles, and let them lie a year before using.

497. Bilberry Wine.

Boil three pints of water with four quarts of selected bilberries for twenty minutes, strain the juice through canton flannel, cover, and let it stand for half an hour; then fill it carefully into another pot; let it boil once more a few seconds with twelve ounces of sugar, one-eighth of an ounce of ground cinnamon, and one-tenth of an ounce of ground cloves; bottle after cooling, seal the bottles, and put them in the cellar.

498. English Blackberry Wine.

Put any large quantity of ripe and dry blackberries in a large stone jar, pour over it boiling water, and place it over night in a tepid oven; squeeze the berries thoroughly in the morning, strain through a fine sieve, and let the juice ferment a fortnight; then add to each four quarts of juice one pound of pulverized sugar, and half a pint of brandy or rum; fill the fluid into a cask, bung well, and let it lie in a cellar a few months before using.

147

499. Cider.

Cider is chiefly produced in large quantities by pressing apples with an addition of water; yet one may obtain smaller quantities for the family use without too great trouble, by grating fine, juicy peeled apples on a grater; filter the juice through a cloth, pour it into stone jars, and add some roasted apples to hasten fermentation. When, after a couple of days, a skin appears on the juice, fermentation is complete; remove the skin, bottle the cider, and keep it in a cool place.

Larger quantities of cider are obtained by mashing good, juicy apples; press them, and fill the juice into a small Rhine wine cask. Place this cask in a cool room upon a skid, when the juice will soon begin to ferment; fermentation will take about a fortnight; during this time remove with a clean piece of linen all stuffs thrown to the surface; as soon as fermentation is done fill the cask up with water, bung it well, and let it lie in the cellar half a year; decant it into another cask, let it lie for another two months, and fill into bottles.

500. Currant Wine.

Collect the perfectly ripe currants on a sunny day, clean, and put them in a big earthen or wooden pot, and mash them with a wooden masher; let ferment in a cellar, and strain through a hair-sieve with a wooden spoon; never use your hands; decant into a little cask; add to each quart of juice half a pound of powdered sugar, and to each twelve quarts of juice one quart of brandy or arrack; let the wine stand six weeks, bottle, and use after two months.

501. Currant Wine in the English Style.

From twelve to fourteen quarts of currants are mashed, the juice pressed out, and the remnants covered with eighteen quarts of cold water; stir repeatedly, press out again the following day, mix with the juice, and fourteen pounds of loaf-sugar; when the sugar is dissolved, fill the juice into a cask, so as not to fill it entirely; bung, and bore a small hole with a gimlet; let it stand four weeks in a place where the temperature never sinks below 68° F.

After this period add three pounds of sugar dissolved in two quarts of warm water; shake the cask well, and bung again. Six or eight weeks later, when no more noise of the fermentation can be heard going on, decant, add two quarts of brandy; let the wine stand two months in the cellar; then fill into another, but not new cask, which must be entirely filled, and bung. After three or four years, always in a temperature not below 68° F., bottle, and you obtain a delicious beverage, which much resembles good grape wine.

502. English Dandelion Wine.

Pluck about four quarts of the yellow petals of the dandelion blossoms; take care that they are clean from insects; infuse them three days in four and a half quarts of hot water; stir it now and then, strain through flannel, and boil the water half an hour with the rind of a lemon and of an orange, some ginger, and three and a half pounds of lump-sugar; after boiling add the lemon and orange, cut into slices, without seeds; let it get cool; add a little yeast on toast. After one or two days the fermentation is done; then fill into a cask and after two months you may bottle.

(The wine is very good against liver-complaints.)

503. Elder Wine.

Twenty-six pounds of elderberries are boiled in fifty quarts of water, an hour, while adding one ounce of pimento and two ounces of ginger; place forty-four pounds of sugar in a tub, strain the fluid over it, squeeze all the juice out of the berries, add four ounces of cremor tartari; let the fluid stand two days, fill into a cask, place a brick over the bung-hole, and stir every other day.

When fermentation is complete, add two or three quarts of cognac spirits; bung, and bottle after four months.

504. Ginger Wine.

Boil sixteen pounds of sugar and twelve ounces of well-pulverized Jamaica ginger in twenty-four quarts of water half an hour; skim carefully, and let it stand till the following day.

Cut seven pounds of raisins in pieces, remove the seeds, put the raisins in a cask with four quarts of good brandy or arrack, and three or four lemons, sliced and without seeds: pour over it the fluid, which you decant carefully; bung the cask; clear the wine after a fortnight with one ounce of pale white glue, and bottle after another fortnight.

505. Gooseberry Wine.

Unripe, but otherwise perfectly developed gooseberries of a good kind are mashed in a tub; after twenty-four hours decant the juice; infuse the berries in lukewarm water twelve hours in the proportion of one quart of water to four quarts of berries; strain; mix it with the decanted juice; add to each twenty quarts of fluid twelve pounds of broken sugar, and let the wine ferment in a warm place. After two or three days fill into a cask; add to each twenty quarts of wine two quarts of best brandy; bung well, and place it in not too cold a cellar; to obtain an excellent gooseberry wine it ought to remain in the cellar five years, yet you may decant after a year: of course the product will be inferior.

506. Sparkling Gooseberry Wine.

Forty pounds of large, but still green gooseberries are mashed in a tub, infused in eighteen quarts of lukewarm water; stir thoroughly; decant the water, and squeeze the fruits through a sieve, while you mix it again with four or five quarts of water.

Dissolve thirty pounds of loaf-sugar, and three and one-third ounces of cremor tartari in the juice, and add water to have altogether fifty quarts of fluid: cover the tub with a cloth, and let it stand undisturbed two days in a temperature not below 60° F.

Then pour the wine into a cask containing exactly 45 or 46 quarts, and keep the remaining fluid for the purpose of filling up afterward during fermentation; when you can no longer hear the hissing noise of fermentation, bung, but make a hole beside the bung with a gimlet, closed by a small cork, which is to be taken out every other day to avoid bursting. After ten or twelve days cork solidly; place the cask in a cool cellar, and let it lie till the end of December; decant the wine into a new cask, and clear with pale white glue in the proportion of one ounce to one quart of wine.

In spring bottle at the time when the gooseberries of the same kind begin to bloom; fasten your corks with wire.

507. Honey Wine à la Russe.

Refine four pounds of honey, and mix it with two pounds of pulverized sugar, the rind of four lemons rubbed on sugar, and the juice of six lemons; after cooling mix it well with eight quarts of cold well-water; pour the fluid into a cask, bung it, and put it in the cellar. After a fortnight decant, bottle, cork, and seal, and let the bottles lie a few weeks before using.

508. Lemon Wine.

Boil six quarts of water with four pounds of lump-sugar to the consistency of syrup; peel five lemons, and put the rind in a large, clean pot; pour the boiling syrup over the rind; when the syrup is cool add the juice of ten lemons, a piece of toast covered with a spoonful of yeast, and let it stand two days, when fermentation begins. Then remove the rind; pour the fluid into a cask which must be completely filled; let the wine ferment, and cork when the fermentation is complete. After three months bottle and use.

509. Orange Wine.

Boil twenty-eight pounds of loaf-sugar in thirty-two quarts of water, with the whites and the cracked shells of four eggs, the whites being beaten to foam; skim well; let the concoction get cool; add the juice of ninety bitter oranges; mix all very well; filter; add half a pound of yeast put on toast, let stand for twenty-four hours; fill into a cask, add one quart of fine brandy. After fermentation is complete, bung well; after three months decant into another cask, add another quart of brandy, let it lie for a year, bottle, and let the bottles lie for three months before using.

510. Pear Champagne.

Juicy and sweet pears are mashed; press the juice out, and fill it into a small cask; cover the bung-hole with a piece of muslin, and let it stand for a few days. The juice begins now to ferment, and to foam considerably; after the fermentation is complete fill into another cask, bung well, and let it lie in a cellar for six weeks; after this fill the wine into bottles, fasten the corks with wire, and you may use it after three or four more weeks.

511. Raisin Wine.

Pour twenty-four quarts of boiling water over twenty-four pounds of extra good raisins; add six pounds of sugar; let it stand a fortnight; stir daily; decant the fluid, squeeze the raisins, and add three-fourths of a pound of finely pulverized cremor tartari; fill into a cask, let it ferment; bung; let it lie for six months, decant into another cask; let it lie again three months, and bottle.

512. Another.

If you wish a raisin wine resembling in taste the muscatel wine you proceed as follows:

Boil eight pounds of choice raisins in twenty-four quarts of water perfectly soft, press them through a sieve, add the mass to the water in which the raisins have been boiled, likewise add twelve pounds of lump-sugar; when the sugar is dissolved let the wine ferment in a cask by adding one-fourth of a quart of yeast. When the fermentation is nearly over, hang a linen bag filled with two and a half quarts of elderberries into the cask; remove the bag as soon as the wine has the required taste; let the wine lie for six months and bottle.

513. Raisin Wine in the Hebrew Style.

The raisin wine, which is used as so-called Easter wine during the Passover in all orthodox Hebrew families, is easily made as follows:

A fortnight before the feast, select three pounds of fine raisins; cut them in small pieces and remove the seeds; put them with one pound of sugar in a jug and pour over six or seven quarts of cold water; place the vessel, covered, on or behind the hearth; skim after three or four days; filter through a funnel lined with linen or blotting-paper into bottles; add to each bottle some stick cinnamon, lemon-peel, and cloves; cork well and put them in the cellar, until you use them.

514. Raspberry Wine.

Ripe raspberries are mashed with a wooden spoon and put into a stone jar; add one quart of cold water to each quart of berries. The following day you decant the fluid, press the berries through a cloth, add one pound of sugar to every quart of wine; fill the wine into a cask and stir daily; when fermentation is done, add one quart of white wine to every four quarts of raspberry wine; bung the barrel, let it lie three months, bottle the wine and it is ready for use.

515. English Raspberry Wine.

Throw twenty quarts of ripe raspberries into a tub, pour twenty quarts of boiling water over them, cover the tub well and let it stand until the following day; skim, press the berries through a hair-sieve and let the fluid stand again from four to five hours. Decant it into a barrel, add gradually twelve pounds of pulverized sugar, mix one quart of the fluid with three table-spoonfuls of very fresh ale yeast and mix this with the rest of the wine; cover the bung-hole with a piece of paper and a brickstone and let the wine ferment. As soon as the fermentation is over, bung the barrel well, and after four weeks decant the wine into another clean barrel; clear the fluid with two-thirds of an ounce of pale, sweet glue and add one quart of fine brandy to the wine; bung well and let it lie for a year in a cool cellar; bottle and seal, and let the bottles lie for another year.

516. Sloe Wine.

Fresh, ripe sloes are put in a tub, for each quart of sloes one quart of water; boil the water and pour it boiling over the sloes; let that stand five days; stir daily. Add to each quart of fluid one pound of loaf-sugar; dissolve by continually stirring; fill all in a cask, add one pint of brandy to each six quarts of fluid; let it lie in the cask for a year, at least, before bottling; let the bottles lie for another year, when the wine will have the goût of port wine.

517. Spiced Wine.

Wash one-fourth of an ounce of cloves, as much ginger, twice as much cinnamon and nutmeg; pour over it ten or twelve quarts of Madeira and let it stand for a few days in moderate warmth; strain it through blotting-paper and drink it in very small doses.

518. Strawberry Wine.

Pour over twelve quarts of strawberries twelve quarts of cold water and let stand twenty-four hours. Strain, add eight pounds of sugar, eight quarts of apple cider, the thin peel of a lemon and one ounce of cremor tartari; fill all in a barrel; it must occupy not more than three-fourths of the barrel's volume; bung, and bore a hole beside the bung with a gimlet; let the barrel stand four weeks on a temperate place. Then add three pounds of sugar, shake the barrel well and bung again. After six to eight weeks decant, add one quart of cognac, fill back the wine into the cleaned barrel, place it two months in the cellar; after this time decant into a smaller cask, which must be filled entirely; bung well; bottle after three years and use.

519. Wischniak.

(CHERRY WINE WITH HONEY À LA RUSSE.)

Into a strong little cask, well bound with iron bands, you fill ripe sour cherries, so that only about two inches room is left; then pour slowly over the cherries clean, white, unboiled honey containing no particles of wax, and fill each empty space between the cherries with honey. As soon as the upper layer of cherries is nearly covered by honey, put the cover tightly on the cask, bung and seal well bung-hole and lid, or best cover the entire surface with pitch to prevent any air from entering; then sink the cask in sand or earth for three months; during this time the fermentation is going on; there is great danger the cask might burst, unless it be of very strong material. After three months the wine is filtered, bottled, and is ready for use.